Contents

Acknowledgments

I was watching a one-woman show on television, and I thought *What a good job she did. This is so well written and directed. This is a great one-woman show.*

Then I saw the credits and discovered that the only way to create a one-woman show is to have a lot of people backstage.

I would like to gratefully acknowledge and thank the people who are part of *The Creative Life*.

The Producers

My husband, Tim, listened, read, comforted and led creatively, graciously and kindly. Our son, Henry, was extremely patient while Mommy used his computers.

My mom baby-sat and typed and baby-sat some more while my dad drove and provided frequent-flyer miles for wilderness retreats. And, of course, Helen and Charles, what a great family we have.

Gramps and Grandma Bass took care of me, fed my family and gave me breaks to write and write and write.

The Directors

Our first women-artists group got the ball rolling: Stacy, Peggy, Robin, Kay, Vicki, Bettie Ann, Diana, Laura and Morgan from long distance.

The women on the staff of Northland Church gave the book its first test drive.

The Technical Directors

Becky Hunter, Lon Garber, Stephanie Royse, Eleanor Tracey, Teresa Lee, Vernon Rainwater and Clare Sera provided red pens and enthusiastic encouragement with each draft.

The Stage Managers

Kathy Wallace got me where I needed to be on time and provided retreat centers, lunches and general motivation.

Dr. Joel Hunter, my pastor, and Julie West, my Bible Study Fellowship teaching leader, continue to strengthen me in the Word of God.

The Set Designers
The Olde Hearthe Bakery in Casselberry provided scones, coffee and a place to sit for hours without interruption.

Tim Tracey and the worship staff at Northland Church gave me a backdrop of faith, fellowship, worship and art.

Randy, Rachel, Sean and the staff of the *Drama Ministry* newsletter gave me another place to speak and mentor church artisans and volunteers.

The Running Crew
Shellie Arnold heeded God's voice and invited me to come to the Florida Christian Writer's Conference where Janis Whipple and Rachel Hoyer welcomed me into the world of writing.

Cindy Bunch and InterVarsity Press challenged me to write this book. Their patience and guidance were a gift to their new author.

The World Showcase Players at Walt Disney's Epcot Center and the cast of *Murder She Wrote* at Universal Studios Florida provided support and opportunities for artistic growth, and they furnished many of my stories.

Clare Sera, my accountability partner of ten years, kept me going by challenging and rewarding me.

There you have it, ladies and gentlemen, the full cast of *The Creative Life*. Take a bow. The crowd goes wild.

Introduction

Creative Possibilities: Getting Ready

> I'm ready, God, so ready
>
> ready from head to toe.
>
> Ready to sing.
>
> Ready to raise a God-song:
>
> "Wake, soul! Wake, lute!
>
> Wake up, you sleepyhead sun!"
>
> I'm thanking you, God, out in the streets,
>
> singing Your praises in town and country.
>
> PSALM 108:1-3 THE MESSAGE

*W*HEN MY BROTHER WAS A TOWHEADED TODDLER, he would leap out of bed before six o'clock, run to my parents' room and announce that it was time for breakfast. To remind Charlie of the proper time for waking up, my mom drew a picture of a clock with the big hand on the twelve and the little hand on the seven and pasted it on his wall. Somehow this connected with Charlie, and from then on only when the real clock struck seven would his door fly open. But if you ask my mother if she is creative, she will point to me.

My dad is the same way. He served in Vietnam, as naval attaché to Sweden and as captain of a destroyer, yet he considers the rest of us the creative ones. He acts as though his career was such a great fit for his personality and abilities that it must not have required imagination. Besides, he says, "Alice is the out-there actress type."

Even my coworkers are in on the conspiracy.

"I am interested in your book even though I'm not the creative type," said my friend who runs the missions program at a large church. I was standing in her home, watching as she selected which beautiful multicultural Christmas ornament to set on each table. The smell of sweet-potato casserole was wafting in from the kitchen, making me anxious for the other guests to arrive.

"Is it possible to run a missions program without being creative?" I teased. We laughed when we thought about the many creative opportunities she encountered daily.

My Creative Journey

Even I, the supposed artsy one, often consider myself an intruder in the creative-types crowd.

When I was a theater major in college my leading man observed, "You know, you don't come alive until there is an audience."

Oh no, I thought, *it can't be true. If I'm not "alive" during rehearsal, that means I'm not creative. Rehearsal is supposed to be the idea part of the process, and I offer nothing until opening night.*

The death knell came when a visiting professor sat in on rehearsal. "You just need to loosen up during the process, be more . . . creative."

I wanted to quit. I knew I was not creative. Indeed, I thought I was a terrible actor and a horrible person.

My creative spark was lit once we opened the show. When I heard the audience breathing and laughing, it fed my energy. But that was clearly not good enough for me; I had to be more creative during rehearsal. I showed up an hour early, warmed up, did aerobics, sang songs, and tried yoga-like stretches. By the time rehearsal started I was exhausted. So I went the opposite direction: I showed up late, did not learn my lines, tried to operate off-the-cuff and make up my character as we went along. That just became irritating.

I finally came to the conclusion that it was hopeless. I was destined to be an uncreative actor who did not come alive until opening night.

Then I graduated and joined a comedy troupe that performed shows at theme parks and festivals—twenty-minute comedy versions of classic plays involving audience-participation. They picked audience members out of the crowd and cast them as Romeo or Juliet. In college we would rehearse for six weeks and perform for two. At my new job we rehearsed for a day and performed five times a day, five days a week. Maybe I could be creative after all!

Because I came alive when the audience was there, I thought I would fit in to the comedy troupe quickly, but it took time. At first I was terrified about picking an audience member, frightened by the lack of control. I watched the other performers to see how they did it. How were they so creative? They listened to the audience and made eye contact with individuals. They were unafraid to share their own personalities and humor, and they were unthreatened by the audience members' contributions. Each offering from the audience was treated as a wonderful gift: "How can we use this gift and enjoy it?"

I was tentative at first, but as I became sure of what I had to offer, my relationship with the audience grew, and I looked forward to their offerings. The most wonderful moment for me came when my partner and I were performing in Michigan. As I told the story, our slightly off version of Camelot, Andy went into the crowd to find our king. He spotted a cute, smiling man with a funny hat. As Andy placed the crown on the man's head, the man raised a microphone to his throat, placed it at his voice box and said, "Do you still want me?"

It was then that we noticed that the funny hat was covering wisps of hair and a shiny pate, licked nearly clean by recent chemotherapy. Andy, who had beaten non-Hodgkins lymphoma, threw his arms around our beaming king. "You bet we want you."

Bolstered by our respect of him, our king raised his microphone several times to offer jokes and a running commentary on the show. The audience was in stitches. We gave him as much support and space as we could, trying to communicate "Yes, we want you! Yes, we want your humor and your creativity. Yes, we want to hear from you!"

The end of that twenty minutes was bittersweet joy. In every show we looked for opportunities for this kind of communion, and now we had seen it. We had taken the chance, and we rejoiced in a moment fulfilled.

It is impossible to wave a magic wand so that you can be more creative. Only God creates something out of nothing. Our creativity comes from within a context, the context of our life as a creation of God, who is the Author and Perfecter, the Artist. From within that context we can unearth what we have to offer, and we can learn to be available to the creative offerings around us.

Now my mission as an actor is not to be more creative. I do what I do because I want people to experience Christ. I want to jump into their lives and surprise them with the stirring in their own hearts. Sometimes they make the connection to Christ and sometimes they do not. Either way my creative life is making the ground fertile for God's revelation, whether I am acting in a twenty-minute audience participation show at a theme park, a full-length Shakespearean drama or a five-minute sketch before a sermon; whether I am offering encouragement to my son's teachers, sharing a cup of coffee with a good friend or greeting my husband when he comes home from work.

Your Creative Journey

This is not a book about actors or poets or painters. *The Creative Life* is about you, whether you consider yourself an artist or not. Every day you have the opportunity to offer something of yourself, your ideas, your perspective, the work of your hands. And every day you are taking in the offerings of others. Creativity is a big part of your life. This book will help you to explore God's design for your creative life.

In this book you will find exercises that are designed to help you explore your imagination and establish an environment for creativity. You may want to use the exercises for daily study and meet in a group weekly, or you may want to linger over the exercises on your own. If you are leading a group, you will find further help in the leader's guide at the back of the book.

Because the workbook is designed to unearth your individual creative life, each person will connect with different exercises. You may want to zip through some and stay with others. Included in each chapter are instructions and introductions for the exercises, along with my stories of discovery. Use the space on the exercise pages to write in your own stories. Because each one of us is unique, I wish you could turn the book back into me so that I could read about your creative life. Instead, I encourage you to write your responses for you, so that you can see how God creatively speaks to and through you.

Each chapter is divided into five parts so that you can cover it in a week, one half-hour each weekday. But feel free to use shorter or longer chunks of time according to your needs. Take as long as you want to go through each chapter, and don't feel pressured to stay on a schedule or to do everything in the book. Instead, be aware of the places where God is calling you to pause or where he is encouraging you to move forward. These may be growth points. The following icons distinguish exercises you will find in each chapter.

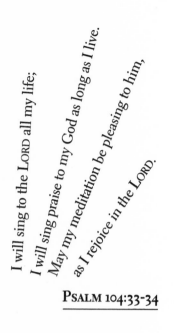

I will sing to the LORD all my life;
I will sing praise to my God as long as I live.
May my meditation be pleasing to him,
as I rejoice in the LORD.

PSALM 104:33-34

The Bible is the focus of *The Creative Life*. When you take in God's perspective, you begin to see your own creative path. In these sections you dig into God's Word revealed in the Bible to see what God says about creativity. Unless otherwise indicated the Bible quotations are from the New International Version of the Bible.

Explore

In these sections you will apply what we see in the Bible. Journaling on a theme will allow you to discover how God is speaking to you along the way; writing down your thoughts gives you a chance to see your response to his work. In these sections you'll find a set of questions to consider with a space set either after each question or at the end for you to journal your responses.

Journal

Imagine

These exercises give you a chance to explore your imagination within the context of Scripture. When you are focused on God's Word, your creative blocks are removed, and your imagination can be connected to the source of creativity. If you are working with a group, you might want to do these exercises together and share how God is speaking to you.

Experience

Creativity is not a mental game; it requires expression. These sections will give you a chance to respond to God by acting on your imaginings.

Tool

Tools are practical methods for using your creative abilities. They will pop up every few chapters to give you something you can use every day to access your creative life.

Worship

Our most satisfying expression happens when we celebrate God for who he is. You will find quotes and Bible verses on the perimeter of the pages and in call-out boxes. These are to remind you that creativity comes from within the context of your relationship to God. In each chapter a Worship section offers a prayer or song suggestions.

Worship is the place of inspiration. All of the Imagine exercises were developed during times of worship. Worship transforms our thinking, putting us in a receptive mode. Use the songs suggested, singing them out loud in your car or just letting them move through your mind. If you are meeting as a group, you can open and close by worshiping together.

On Your Way

Just like we wanted the king in our Michigan show, God wants you. He values you, and he values your personality, your humor, your offering and your creativity. God values you even though you are sure that you are too ravaged by the cancer of sin to make an offering.

What bravery it took that man to lift his microphone and ask, "Do you still want me?" And it will take bravery for you to experience your imagination. This book will give you the support and the space you need to look for, participate in and rejoice in your creative life.

In each chapter we will look at our own fears and discover new tools for exploring our imagination so that our creative life can become a playground, a place to experience and express the glory of God.

To get ready, worship God for his greatness. Invite the Lord to prepare the way for you to unearth your creativity so that you will grow closer to him.

Read this psalm aloud:

Praise the LORD, I tell myself;
 O LORD my God, how great you are!
You are robed with honor and with majesty;
 you are dressed in a robe of light.
You stretch out the starry curtain of the heavens;
 you lay out the rafters of your home in the rain clouds.
You placed the world on its foundation
 so it would never be moved.
Mountains rose and valleys sank
 to the levels you decreed.
Then you set a firm boundary for the seas,
 so they would never again cover the earth. (Psalm 104:1-3, 5, 8-9 NLT)

Or you may sing one of these hymns:
"Glorify Thy Name"
"How Great Thou Art"
"Come, Thou Almighty King"

Worship

"It might reasonably be maintained that the true object of all human life is play. Earth is a task garden; heaven is a playground."

G. K. CHESTERTON

Chapter 1

Creative Foundation: Restoring the Divine Connection

Jesus answered, "I am the way and the truth and the life. No one comes to the Father except through me. If you really knew me, you would know my Father as well. From now on, you do know him and have seen him."

JOHN 14:6-7

WE ALL HAVE A SNAPSHOT IN OUR MIND OF WHO is creative and who is not. Under the "not" category we secretly put businesspeople, mothers, computer specialists, telemarketers and Christians. In this way we limit our definition of creativity to artistic expression. Creativity is a necessary ingredient of art, but it is also required for life. How much imagination does it require to get through a job interview? Or listen to coworkers' complaints? Or explain to your kids why they can't watch HBO after nine o'clock in the evening? What about being in this world and not of it? We all need tons of creativity, and creativity is available to all of us at all times.

The foundation for our creativity is our Creator. Because we are made in the image of God, our creativity and our faith are intertwined. To enjoy a creative life we need to be free to experience more of Christ's inspiration and less of our own inhibitions, fears and sin patterns. We live a creative life in response to the Lord Jesus as he is revealed

"The Bible is a love story. It began in time but exists outside of all boundaries of time and space, in eternity. The Bible is the story of your life. It's why you search through your life to find the perfect counterpart. It's why you feel alone, disconnected, misunderstood. It's why at times you feel a sudden joy, or an indescribable longing. You are destined for eternal fulfillment. This true story is why you dream."

CLARE SERA,
EASTER: THE LOVE STORY

in the Scriptures and by the Holy Spirit.

Creative Nature

Watching my women's group break for coffee, I was fascinated by how carefully each of the women chose just the right cup. It was as if they were thinking, *Which one expresses me right now? Who am I today, the tailored tan teacup with an elegant black stripe? Or the 70s earthenware with a single rose? Maybe the cobalt blue with gold stars.*

The image of the eternal in us makes us want to express ourselves in the details. We were made for heaven, and once we get there, our joy will be complete. The pleasures of heaven will take us beyond our five senses and fulfill all of who we were created to be.

But even as we are reaching for the perfect cup, we pull back our hand. *(Did someone see me? I shouldn't express myself with a cup! How silly.)* We stop wanting to express our uniqueness because we are trapped in our flesh. And yet it is the eternal One who has encased us in these bodies. Imagine the pleasure of our heavenly Father when we delight in choosing a coffee cup. He must love it when we experience the richness of his world, a world that will fade. We will not need to choose the right cup in heaven because we will be fully expressed, fully known. But that does not mean our life here is for naught. We are his creatures and he delights in us. So go ahead, choose a cup, touch a smooth stone, sing joyfully off key!

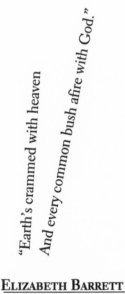

*"Earth's crammed with heaven
And every common bush afire with God."*

ELIZABETH BARRETT
BROWNING

Explore

Let's look at the nature of God and our relationship to his creativity.
❑ Read Genesis 1:26-27 and 2:19-20. How was humanity created?

❑ What was the model for humanity's creation?

❏ Describe the events of Genesis 2:19 as if you were in Adam's place.

❏ What do you think the task of naming the animals required of Adam?

❏ Now compare those verses with Job 39:13-18. What is beautiful about the ostrich?

❏ What is unique about her?

❏ What is she lacking?

❏ How do you feel about the ostrich after reading this passage?

❏ What is the difference between God's relationship to the ostrich and his relationship to Adam?

Journal

❑ When have you felt that you were in close communion with God?

❑ How is creativity part of your relationship with God?

Conversation and Communion

In the beginning
God created the heavens
and the earth.
The earth was empty,
a formless mass cloaked
in darkness. And the Spirit
of God was hovering
over its surface.
Then God said,
"Let there be light,"
and there was light.

GENESIS 1:1-3 NLT

Creativity is part of our nature; we, not the ostrich, have been given the ability to create. God breathes life into our dusty forms. His Spirit hovers over us, calling to the depths and leading us into abundant living. We are creative because we are made in God's image.

Imagination is part of our nature: we solve problems, we relate to others, we come up with ideas, we make guesses, we are resourceful, we dream and fantasize. Close your eyes and imagine Adam's process of naming the animals. He was not randomly picking names out of a hat. Names and language did not previously exist before Adam began (and he probably did not have a hat). Adam made those names up by looking at the animals, assessing them, seeing how they related to each other and what they did. Adam was not alone; he was in perfect communion and conversation with God. It was not Adam's idea to be the namer of the animals; it was God's desire for Adam to be involved. Once he was invited to name the animals, Adam looked very deeply into the character of each one before he labeled it and sent it away. Close your eyes again and try to picture God bringing Adam the tall, funny bird that runs faster than a horse, and Adam crying out "Ostrich!" What a scene.

When you use your imagination, you are putting into play your experiences, personality, abilities and intuition. Your relationship with God gives you insight into his purposes and his creative process. Your creativity is a link to the living God.

I was in my early twenties when I recommitted my life to Christ, and I immediately placed tremendous pressure on myself to conform to my image of a Christian woman. I thought my hair would need to pouf and my Bible would need to sprout lace, and I hoped that I would be overcome by the urge to wear a pinafore. I knew what a Christian woman looked like, and I didn't look like that.

Describe your image of the perfect Christian.

My perfect Christian man wears glasses, of course. Just this side of computer nerd, he is neat and looks freshly scrubbed. He has short hair, he wears a plaid shirt, and his hand is extended, ready to shake. His Bible is unobtrusive but at the ready. He looks like he doesn't have a care in the world.

My perfect Christian woman wears a blue floral dress with a pressed white collar. She does not have graham cracker handprints on her skirt, even though she does have a toddler by the hand (homeschooled), a baby in a backpack (breast-fed, on a schedule) and is picking up her elementary-school child from the private Christian school. Her shiny brown hair is neatly pulled back, and without a bit of makeup her face is radiant.

Stereotypes put pressure on us. They stop us from thinking and imagining the possibilities. By examining a snapshot of how you think you are supposed to be, you can break through that creative block.

Because of the stereotype that I held when I recommitted my life to Christ, I struggled with my creativity. How could my two worlds possibly come together? I struggled with doing plays that weren't about Jesus. I even worried about working in the drama ministry with my husband. Just how creative should I be when I write a script or act in a sketch? Surely as a Christian I should be listening to God instead of using my imagination.

But what if our imagination is a gift from God? And if it

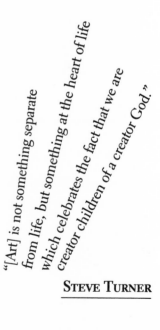

"[Art] is not something separate from life, but something at the heart of life which celebrates the fact that we are creator children of a creator God."

STEVE TURNER

is, what if using our imagination is a way to hear from him?

In order to continue in my vocation I had to know what God says about imagination. Not just for me but also for the nonbelievers I was working with in the theater. I wanted to tell them that God is interested in them, that he values their creativity and their artistry. And I wanted to tell the people in the church who were struggling with their originality and imagination that their expression is as valuable as that of a famous artist. Being creative is part of our nature as human beings.

Recovering the Design

When I was in college, I read books telling me to recapture my creativity by harnessing my inner child; after all, it was said, children are so creative, and they have no inhibitions. I remember in my childhood bouncing between fanciful play and hiding out in the school clinic every time an oral presentation was due. Sure, I was more willing to tap into my creative abilities when I was a child, just as my fears and inhibitions were equally available to me.

If as children we were all free to be creative, then why as adults do we think that creativity is only for certain people? From the beginning we have been connected to God and to each other; from dust we are made in his image, his breath bringing us life and bone from bone relying on one another. Creativity should flow through us like that breath of life. Then why do experts say we need to go back to being childlike to recover our creativity? Because we did lose our creativity; we lost the original design for our communion with God and each other.

Explore

❏ Read Genesis 2:15-16, 25; 3:1-6; and 3:21-24. From 2:25 describe the relationship between Adam and Eve.

❏ Looking at these verses and at Genesis 1:28, do you think Eve did not know the command recorded in Genesis 2:16-17? Why or why not?

❏ In Genesis 3:3 how does Eve describe God's instructions?

❏ How have you been like Eve in the way you hear and interpret God's instructions?

❏ What is recorded in Genesis 3:6 about what happened next?

❏ Skim chapter 3 of Genesis and record the results of the man and woman's disobedience. In 3:21 how did the Lord respond to their situation?

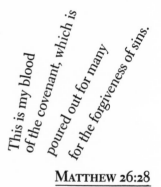

This is my blood of the covenant, which is poured out for many for the forgiveness of sins.

MATTHEW 26:28

❏ What did Adam and Eve lose as a result of their disobedience?

❏ What did they retain?

We need everything to be redeemed. Both Adam and Eve were well aware of God's design for their lives in the garden. They were responsible to act on what they knew, and they chose to ignore that responsibility and to take what seemed pleasing. Because sin entered the world, all that we are and have is under the curse of sin. Our creative abilities are tainted. But they are not taken away. In Genesis 3:20 we are told that Eve would become the mother of all the living. In 3:16 we read that God told her of the pain she would experience as a result of sin, but he did not take away her ability to give birth, to participate in the creation of life. In Adam's curse, God predicted the pain of toil but promised that he would eat as a result of his labors; in toil Adam would continue to produce.

The Life of the Creature

He himself bore our sins
in his body on the tree,
so that we might die to sins
and live for righteousness;
by his wounds you
have been healed.
For you were like sheep going
astray, but now you
have returned
to the Shepherd
and Overseer of your souls.

1 PETER 2:24-25

Our creative nature is under our fallen human nature. This beautiful gift of God is under a curse of toil, pain, dust and shame. It is not surprising then that we experience pride and fear about our creativity. But there is hope. Our creative nature can become a creative life through the redeeming work of Christ. The difference between our creative nature and a creative life is redemption. Our creativity, like everything else in our nature, is redeemed by Christ.

From the Genesis passage we learn that sin bears the curse of death. From our lives we know that this is true, that there is not only physical death but also decay and death in our hearts and spirits. But Peter, Jesus' disciple, says that because Jesus bore the curse of sin and death, we do not have to die. Instead, our sin dies, and we can live for righteousness. We also know from our lives that living for righteousness is impossible for us. Think of your imagination and your creativity. Why have you tried to squelch it in the past? Perhaps because it led you to immorality, hurt, fear, shame or embarrassment, but not to righteousness.

I love the phrase that Peter uses about Jesus the Overseer of our souls. When you come to Jesus, he oversees your soul, your thoughts, your actions, and yes, your creativity. But life in Christ is a not merely a matter of having a good manager checking our work. It is a life in which the sin that had flowed through our veins is replaced with the transfused lifeblood of Jesus.

Your creativity is not something to be discarded because you have experienced sin in it in the past. Rather, your creativity is damaged and it needs to be exchanged. Your creativity will not save you. Saying "I'm an artist" or "I'm creative" will not purify you. Everything in us needs to be redeemed by Christ, including our creativity.

If you have received Christ, dedicate your creativity to him by praying this prayer aloud:

Experience

Almighty and eternal God, so draw our hearts to *thee*, so guide our minds, so fill our imaginations, so control our wills, that we may be wholly *thine*, utterly dedicated unto *thee*; and then use us, we pray *thee*, as *thou wilt*, and always to *thy* glory and the welfare of *thy* people; through our Lord and Savior Jesus Christ. *Amen*. (Collect 61. A Prayer of Self-Dedication, *The Book of Common Prayer*)

If you are not sure whether you have invited Jesus into your life, if you cannot remember a specific experience with him and you are beginning to see that you need him, you are right. Knowing Jesus is the most vital thing in your life. To recognize God as more than just a big entity high above us, you need to acknowledge that Christ is the Savior and that you need his saving grace. Pray:

Gracious God,
our sins are too heavy to carry,
too real to hide,
and too deep to undo.
Forgive what our lips tremble to name,
what our hearts can no longer bear,
and what has become for us
a consuming fire of judgement.
Set us free from a past that we cannot change;
open to us a future in which we can be changed;
and grant us grace
to grow more and more in your likeness and image;
through Jesus Christ, the light of the world. *(The Book of Common Worship)*

For the life of a creature
is in the blood,
and I have given it to you
to make atonement
for yourselves on the altar;
it is the blood that makes
atonement for one's life.

Leviticus 17:11

Receiving Christ means confessing that we are sinners and asking him to purify us. Then he will come and live in our hearts and change us.

A Warm Room

I had been a Christian for four years when my counselor told me that I didn't like to "share my heart." Well, I was furious. I stomped out and was sure I'd never talk to the counselor again. What was he talking about? I shared my opinion all the time, and I had friends. Two or three friends. Only one of them really knew me, and sometimes I surprised her with my dreams. "I would never have guessed that about you" was something I heard often.

The next Sunday during worship, I asked God to show me my heart. An image popped into my head of a room in which the ceiling, walls and floor were made out of hardwood. The wood was light in color, and it was varnished so that it shined. There were no windows, and the room was so empty that I could hear the click of my heels echoing as I walked. I knew from that sound that I was in my heart's room. It was such a sad sound to me, heels clicking. Sad but familiar. In school my friends had dubbed me "student actress on the go" because I was on so many committees. I was always running from one thing to the next, never allowing time for interaction, just accomplishment. I knew that my counselor was right: I didn't share my heart.

I could tell that Jesus was in that room because it was warm and inviting. But the room was closed up and empty, save for the presence of my dear Savior. Who else but he would sit in an empty room waiting for his beloved?

Imagine

"Here I am! I stand at the door and knock. If anyone hears my voice and opens the door, I will come in and eat with him and he with me" (Revelation 3:20).

After you read this verse from Revelation, close your eyes, relax into your chair and take a deep breath. As you breathe in, feel that breath going into your shoulders and arms, allowing tension to be released. Breathe in again, and think on the Revelation verse. Imagine that the door is the door to the room of your heart. Now picture your heart's door.

What does it look like? Is it made of wood, and does it have a latch? Is it a screen porch door? Or a stone door with a peephole?

What does it feel like to the touch?

What would it feel like to approach the door from the outside?

Now, open the door and describe the room.

What are the colors and textures in the room?

Is Jesus there? If so, is he comfortable? How has he made himself at home? Has he rearranged the room at all?

You can end your heart-room imagining by singing one of these hymns:

"Open the Eyes of My Heart"

"Just As I Am"

"Create in Me a Clean Heart"

Or try personalizing John 15:5 and making it your prayer this week. "I am the vine; you are the branches. If a man remains in me and I in him, he will bear much fruit; apart from me you can do nothing."

If you have Jesus living in your heart, that means the creative spark, the Word, is in there! The creative life is Jesus. With Christ living in our hearts we have access to abundant creativity. We do not create out of nothing as he does. Instead we are grafted into him, and our creativity comes from him and produces eternal fruit.

Worship

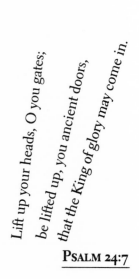

Lift up your heads, O you gates; be lifted up, you ancient doors, that the King of glory may come in.

PSALM 24:7

Chapter 2

Creative Instrument: Life as His Image

> For you created my inmost being;
>
>> you knit me together in my mother's womb.
>
> I praise you because I am fearfully and wonderfully made;
>
>> your works are wonderful,
>
>> I know that full well.
>
> PSALM 139:13-14

WHEN YOU READ A BOOK, PERHAPS YOU PICTURE the characters. As your eyes glide down the page, images of the action appear in the background of your mind. When you are listening to music, the melody and the lyrics weave themselves together and conjure up pictures in your imagination.

Our creativity is available to us all the time. We use it constantly, so much so that we don't always realize it. I was leading a group of Christian artists, and Katie, a singer, actor, piano teacher, mom and wife, was overwhelmed by her experience with God that encouraged her creativity. "I never thought I was, but in my prayer time he affirmed that I am creative!" How did she miss out on her creativity in all of those roles? Certainly you and I look at her life and think, "Wow, she is much more creative than I am."

In your heart's-room exercise some of you may have experienced vivid imaginings. You might have pictured rooms with bright colors, furniture in colorful tapestry, gardens with sprawling vines. One person pictured a room made entirely of food; she entered through the Pop-Tart door and sat on a Jell-O couch!

On the other hand, perhaps you were not immersed in imagery during the exercise. Perhaps, like me, you can imagine some focused point or get a general feeling, but you are not surrounded by detail. Even when you read fiction, maybe you picture the characters, but their surroundings are a shadowy backdrop.

If your imagination exercise failed to evoke colorful detail, resist the urge to label yourself as uncreative. Instead remind yourself of what we discovered in chapter one, that creativity is part of your nature and is redeemed by Christ. Then your creative life becomes filled with light and life.

The first step in our creative journey is to discover not whether we are creative, but how we are creative. With the divine connection to your creative life restored, you can spend your time in this chapter exploring your personal brand of originality.

Have you ever thought that what everyone else does is creative, but not what you do? Me too. I wish that I could make things with my hands, but even my toddler's crayon drawings look better than mine. I can never visualize colors together either. I only buy clothes that I see on a mannequin. I think that people who draw or do crafts or sew or decorate are really creative and that the things I do are ordinary. But the things that are ordinary for me you might consider creative. The things that you enjoy doing and that are part of your life are a revelation to me. Each one of us has our own brand of creativity that adds richness to life.

Originality, creativity and imagination are intimidating words because they come with tremendous responsibility. The dictionary defines creativity as "having or showing the power to produce original work, as in literature." Yep, that's intimidating. If I have to live up to "having the power to produce original work," then I am back to "I am not creative." But creativity permeates our entire day, so we need a definition that applies to daily life. I define creativity as

Memorials

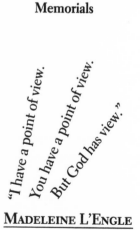

"I have a point of view.
You have a point of view.
But God has view."

MADELEINE L'ENGLE

the availability to a new thought that leads to an expression.

Available is one of my favorite words because it implies readiness. I picture, for example, a man who is available sitting on the edge of his chair at a table in a streetside café. He leans in, ready to hear and move on the offer. I love *openness* too. I picture a woman languishing in an armchair in the back corner of a bookstore coffeehouse, beckoning me to relax there. In this definition of *creativity*, God makes an offer to us, and we, leaning forward, are available to that new thought.

If that new thought came from the Holy Spirit, then your expression reveals the Lord in some small or grand way. That expression also includes an action by you that reveals something about you—about your experience, your personality or your feelings.

Experience

At one time I viewed my life as a series of monuments to sin and shame; I thought I was remembered only by the mistakes I made. Then I read Joshua 4:1-7 and saw how our lives can be full of monuments to the things God has done, memorials of his work.

Read Joshua 4:1-17, and then revisit some of the monuments in your life with a God view. In light of our definition of creativity, look and see if those monuments mark creative moments, moments in which God gave you a new thought or a new direction and you acted on it. When was a time that someone affirmed your creativity? When were you proud of an idea you had? Did you act on the idea?

Make a timeline of your creative moments.

❏ What creative threads do you see woven through your timeline?

❏ Where have those threads led you?

❏ What do your monuments that mark creative moments tell you about God?

❏ What do they tell you about you?

❏ How has God been creatively working in your life?

The Bible is rich with creative expression. It draws on almost every literary style: song, poem, biography, narrative, proverb, prophecy, letters, love story. It is the perfect illustration of how God uses us. The Bible has a beginning, middle and end that are woven together perfectly. It would have been impossible for all of the Bible's contributors to achieve this kind of consistency if there was not a unifying factor, the Holy Spirit, overseeing their souls. Yet the diverse contributors, people like Moses, David, Solomon and Paul, are revealed as individuals. It is beautiful to see the consistency of theme from Genesis to Revelation while

Metaphor

each contributor's personality, life experience and style are fully used by the Author.

Probably because I am a dramatist I love reading the gospel accounts and hearing Jesus' parables. Jesus said, "The kingdom of heaven is like yeast that a woman took and mixed into a large amount of flour until it worked all through the dough" (Matthew 13:33).

When Jesus taught in parables, he was not just being secretive. He used illustrations to engage the imaginations of the listeners. We use parables and metaphors all the time: "The mall was a zoo today!" "My boss? He's a teddy bear."

Illustrations, parables and metaphors give us a picture that we can relate to. Metaphor gets us out of our normal thinking patterns and shakes those dormant synapses in our brains by drawing us into relationship with a concept. Through metaphor an idea becomes something we experience.

Tool

Metaphor is a tool that you can use to engage your imagination and enhance your awareness of your own ideas. To practice look at Matthew 13:33.

How is yeast like the kingdom of God?

❑ When you mix it with flour you can't see it, but you know it's there.

❑ It's available.

❑ It's sprinkled throughout our daily life.

Keep going:

❑

❑

❑

❑

❏

❏

This metaphor can give you a fresh, new and exciting understanding of bread, yeast and the kingdom of heaven! From now on when you smell freshly baked bread, think of the Lord Jesus. Creativity is about relationship; it springs out of our relationship to God and connects us to his work and to his children.

In acting class, actors refer to themselves as instruments. It sounds self-indulgent, but the metaphor is meant to be practical. When a violinist sits down to play, he brings his skill and talent to life through the violin. An actor is an instrument made up of her body, her voice, her experiences, her emotions and her expressions. Her instrument and the script, together with skill and talent, bring a character to life.

I was at acting school in New York when I first became acquainted with this idea. Our acting techniques teacher had us do an exercise that takes a great amount of courage. Each person is to sing a song, one note at a time. You hold that note as long as you can. Then you close your eyes, take a deep breath, start the next note and open your eyes. It is very intimidating to open your eyes and see a group of people staring at you while you bellow at them. You want to roll your eyes and make faces that will say, "This is soooo stupid." Or you want to signal before you start, "I really can sing and this is a great song." There is no way you can "perform" during an exercise like this; you can't pour on the charm or dazzle them with your smile. You just stand there feeling totally naked, hoping you won't die.

My turn came. I was a singer, so I was not bothered by that part of the exercise. I took my place on the stage and closed my eyes. The thought flashed through my mind that I could just run away, but instead I opened my mouth and

Fearfully and Wonderfully Made

my eyes simultaneously. "Myyyyyyyyyyyyyyy." Wow! No one was laughing. No one was making a face. No one hated me because I was making funny noises. It was kind of like skydiving—scary but safe. Deep breath. "Fuuuunnnnnnnnn . . ." The teacher left her seat and circled me. For some reason, that did not distract me. I had seen her do that to the others, so I was expecting it. "Neeeeeeeeeeeyyyyy." Deep breath; she was circling me again. "Vaaaaaalllllllll . . ." Deep breath. She patted my back. I was determined not to look at her. "Eeennnnnnnnnn . . ." Deep breath. There she goes; maybe I will be done soon. "Tiiiiiiiiinnnnnnne."

She rapped her cane on the floor and announced dramatically, "We have quite an instrument here!" I returned to my seat. I understood that it was not my performance that had won the teacher's positive response. She was commenting on my availability to the exercise. I was able to shake free from my own nerves, dismiss the distractions and sing.

It was the first time I realized that I was not my own. I was an instrument. Built for something. This teacher seemed to think I was built to be an actor. At the time, so did I. And I still think one of my roles is to be an actor. But I have a bigger role as an instrument of God. Each of us is being fitted and trained to be part of a heavenly orchestra. Each of us is asked to be available to his filling, to stand our ground, take on our role and be used by him.

You are an instrument; your life is a creative expression of God. He has made you with unique beauty, and there is no one else like you; there never has been, and there never will be again.

> For we are God's workmanship, created in Christ Jesus to do good works, which God prepared in advance for us to do.
>
> EPHESIANS 2:10

Imagine

Yet, O LORD, you are our Father.
 We are the clay, you are the potter;
 we are all the work of your hand. (Isaiah 64:8)

I praise you because I am fearfully and wonderfully made;
 your works are wonderful,
 I know that full well.
My frame was not hidden from you

when I was made in the secret place.
When I was woven together in the depths of the earth,
   your eyes saw my unformed body. (Psalm 139:14-16)

Close your eyes now and take a deep breath. Meditate on the two passages you just read. You are the work of his hand. His works are wonderful, you know that full well.

Now invite your imagination to be available to a new thought; imagine your life as a work of art.

Are you a movie, a book, a painting, a symphony? Are you a story, poem, ballet, tapestry or photograph?

How is God singing through you, expressing himself to the world?

Picture God as the potter. Is it easy for him to mold you or is he having to work the clay?

How is he shaping you as a work of art right now?

What does it look like to be a wonderful work of God's hands?

How does the Artist feel about his work?

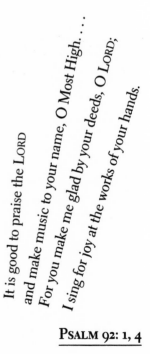

It is good to praise the LORD
and make music to your name, O Most High. . . .
For you make me glad by your deeds, O LORD;
I sing for joy at the works of your hands.

PSALM 92: 1, 4

Each one of us is different. If you are a short story, I am a painting. God is speaking through both of us. He is crafting the story beautifully, with deep characters, funny, poignant scenes and an interesting plot. He is adding texture and color to the painting. When you see a painting you are drawn into the beauty of its strokes and colors, the scene and story of it. And while you are relating to a work of art, enjoying its beauty, moved by its sadness, you are registering something about the painter, the artist, the author. So it is with you and me. God does not bring us into the family and say, "Well, you were a painting and you are a sculpture, but now that you are Christians, I need you all to be poems." You are a symphony, I am a poem, he is a barbershop-quartet melody, she is a sculpture in bronze, and God is expressed through each of us. And God does an amazing thing. He puts all of these works of art together, and they form one perfect picture, the body of the Lord Jesus.

Risk

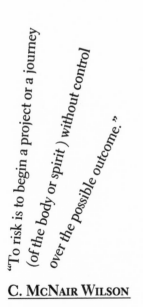

"To risk is to begin a project or a journey (of the body or spirit) without control over the possible outcome."

C. McNair Wilson

Being an instrument involves risk. I discovered that in both of my Bible study groups I always sit in the same place. East side of the room, third person in. It is so ingrained that I didn't even notice I do it. Then one week I walked in the room, and I had an urge to sit directly across from my usual chair. I hesitated. If I sat over there I would not be looking directly at the same faces. Carol and Jennifer's reactions I can handle. But I had no idea what looks Diane and Kathy would give me, plus I wouldn't be able to see the clock and the door. Changing my seat would put me in a more vulnerable position because I would have to be ready for something different. I sat down in my regular seat. I just wasn't ready to move.

When you make yourself available to God you risk your self-image. It feels like he will change you drastically. That is not likely. He will, however, complete the design he has already mapped out. Look back at some of the monuments that mark creative moments in your life, and you will see that he has been expanding your view and fulfilling your abilities and growing you in skill. He doesn't start you out with an interest in sewing then suddenly ask you to be a race car driver. When God asks you to do something you can usually look back and see the seeds of that thing strewn across your life. It only feels like he is taking you in an opposite direction because you had decided what your life should look like. The only thing you have to risk by being a creative instrument of God is your image of yourself. God is secure in his image of you.

The Lord Jesus risked our image of him. We expected him to look and act like our picture of a king, a deliverer of a nation. He came and shattered our demands about what kind of God he should be, and he fulfilled us by being the Savior we need.

Compare Isaiah 53:2-3 and 10-12 with Psalm 139:13-16. What is more attractive: the inmost being or the outer form? Respond from these passages.

Explore

❏ What do you think draws people to the Lord Jesus?

❏ What do you think repels them from him?

❏ What does Isaiah 53:10-11 tell us about the beauty that the Father sees in Jesus?

❏ Isaiah 53:11 in the NKJV reads, "He shall see the labor of His soul, and be satisfied. By His knowledge my righteous servant shall justify many, for He shall bear their iniquities." What causes the Lord Jesus to be satisfied?

❏ Do you see yourself as the labor of God's soul?

Chapter 3

Creative Invitation: Created for Creativity

Give to the LORD the glory due his name;

bring an offering and come into his courts.

Worship the LORD in the splendor of his holiness;

tremble before him, all the earth.

PSALM 96:8-9 NKJV

YOU ARE GOD'S WORKMANSHIP, A UNIQUE CRE-
ation, a work of art. But you were not made to sit on a ped-
estal or to hang on a wall. You are an instrument to be
played by the Artist and enjoyed by the audience. That is
the reason our definition of creativity is practical and artistic. Your life in art is a participatory one. The Artist will inspire you to join him in making choices so that you and all
who see you will enjoy the beauty of his holiness.

Being available to creativity is not as easy as it looks on paper. You already know that because you have risked before.
You handed in your drawing, and it was the only one that the
teacher did not put up on the board. You set aside time to
write the story brewing in your head, only to cancel your personal time for a child who felt too sick to go to school. You
came up with a great idea, but everyone around the conference table stared blankly until someone said, "I don't get it."

Our fears of expression are not unfounded; each of us
has experienced the pain of rejection when we have tried

to put our originality into action.

I sang in the church choir when I was in third grade. I have a deep voice, and even back then it had a husky, Bea Arthur quality. But I could hit some pretty high notes, and my vibrato made it seem like I had a trained voice, so I got to sing soprano. One Easter we were working on a very hard classical piece, and the back row of the soprano section was struggling with the descant. We held up the entire rehearsal so we could work on our part.

"Reach down deep! Come on, you can do this," our director challenged.

We sat up straight and took big belly breaths. I dropped my jaw and let it rip. The tenors were applauding and so were the altos, but they were on the other side of the room. The rest of the soprano section, right in front of me, turned in their seats, mouths agape, looking horrified.

"What's the matter?" I asked, already turning red.

"What was that? You sounded like an opera singer!"

Maybe they meant it as a compliment, but what I heard was, "You sounded different. You sounded like you were trying to sound different." Within a month I had started singing as a second soprano, and the next year I demoted myself to the alto section.

Ask and it will be given to you; seek and you will find; knock and the door will be opened to you.

MATTHEW 7:7

Laughter into Mourning

What happened when you stepped out creatively and read your story to the class? Or showed a drawing to friends? Or submitted your poem to the school newspaper? Or tried out for the choir?

When your offering was rejected, did you laugh and say, "Oh, that silly thing?" then secretly decide that you couldn't draw or sing or write? Did you agree that you are not creative so you could make sure you wouldn't have to go through that again? It is time to turn your self-protective laughter into mourning and to grieve the loss of your creative joy.

"Come near to God and he will come near to you. Wash your hands, you sinners, and purify your hearts, you double-minded. Change your laughter to mourning and your joy to gloom. Humble yourselves before the Lord, and he

Journal

will lift you up" (James 4:8-10).

Describe your experiences of creative rejection.

Mourn the loss of your creative joy by telling God what you miss about expressing yourself creatively in that way:

❑ Lord, I miss coloring outside of the lines.

❑ Lord, I miss getting my hands full of clay.

❑ Lord, I miss singing really loudly.

❑ Lord, I miss paste and construction paper.

❑ Lord, I miss writing bad poetry.

❑ Lord, I miss high school band practice.

❑ Lord, I miss playing in the mud.

Ask God to heal your places of loss or hurt.

❑ Have you experienced redemption of those losses? If so, how did it happen?

The Sound of Walking   Remember we are not the first to feel ashamed of ourselves or embarrassed because of something we did.

❏ Read Genesis 3:8-9. How did the man and woman respond to God after the Fall?

Explore

❏ How did God respond to them?

❏ Have you ever heard God's voice call to you? If so, what did that feel like?

Listen, listen to me, and eat what is good, and your soul will delight in the richest of fare. Give ear and come to me; hear me, that your soul may live.

❏ What was your response?

Isaiah 55:2-3

Tool

Our senses store our responses in a powerful way. Each of us has had an experience of walking along a familiar street as the breeze shifts. You take a deep breath, and the fragrance of a tree transports you back to the summer when you were seven years old, playing under the sprinkler. Our senses are a key that unlocks our experiences and our imagination.

I was working with my husband on a project for church. We were writing monologues, reviewing poetry and picking out songs that would be part of a worship service. After an hour of sitting in front of a blank computer screen, my husband decided to take a drive to clear his mind. I was determined to come up with something creative while he was out. I stared at the screen. Suddenly, I had an urge to make chicken soup. What a great idea! It was raining, and we were both getting over colds. I jumped up and started to work. While the broth was simmering I cut up carrots and questioned God: "Why can't I come up with anything?" The steam warmed my hand as I stirred the soup. Tim came in the door, took one whiff and declared, "Chicken soup! Perfect. I can't imagine a better way to get us thinking." Then the light bulb went on in my mind—I was being creative.

Here's what I experienced: First, God inspired the idea of chicken soup. Then the physical and sensory actions of cutting, stirring, smelling and tasting engaged my mind. Finally, God affirmed my creative abilities through Tim's response. We were renewed and came up with more ideas than one service could hold.

❏ When have you experienced a smell or taste that reminded you of a pleasant event?

❏ What kind of smell or taste or touch or sound brings you comfort?

❏ What kind of activity helps you think?

The sensory description tool comes from the actor's bag of tricks. When an actor is trying to bring reality to a character, he imagines what the character's room looks like, what the character's clothes feel like, what smells are wafting in from the character's kitchen. When an actor is aware of his senses, they help him to relay what he is imagining to the audience. Have you ever seen a movie or play and known just what it would feel like to be in that place with those characters? Visually, you were taking in the images, and through your senses you were remembering what it feels like to be in a small, old, wooden country church or in a crowded airport on Thanksgiving.

Our emotions are strongly connected to our senses. In a college acting class I was asked to sit in a chair, close my eyes and imagine an object in my hand. Then I was to "explore" the imaginary object using my senses. The final step of the exercise was to describe the object using sensory expressions. Four out of five times, an actor would imagine an apple. "It is crisp, red, juicy, tart, cold, smooth." Without a script or a strong context it is hard to access our imagination.

The first time I tried the exercise I couldn't imagine anything in my hand. It seemed too silly. I decided to try again so I wouldn't fail the class. I was determined to clear my mind of preconceived notions. I would not try to imagine an object. I would not worry about whether I was thinking of the "right" object. I would just open my hand and see what my imagination produced.

I closed my eyes and took a deep cleansing breath. I opened my hand. To my total surprise I imagined that there was a button in my palm. I couldn't believe it! I put aside the thought that a button is a dumb object because it has no taste or smell. I rolled the button around in my hand and pressed it on my leg. I wondered where the button had come from. I pictured myself in the closet of the boy I had a crush on. I leafed through his shirts to see if any of them was missing a button. I was disappointed to find that my button was not his. Then I had an image of my dad and me sitting in our rowboat on the lake in Idaho. It was early morning, around five o'clock. A mist was coming off the water, and Dad and I were drinking coffee as we sat in the boat, fishing for trout. I looked at the collar of Dad's fishing shirt, the one he has worn since 1962, and sure enough, there was a button missing.

Our imaginations are a playground, a gift from God that allows us to explore our feelings, memories and ideas. The sensory description tool invites you fully into your imagination. You imagined your heart's door, and you imagined its interior as a room, and you saw your life in art. Here's an opportunity to add the sensory description tool to our Imagine exercises.

Imagine

Read Genesis 3:8-9 again. Close your eyes and relax. Take a deep breath and roll the words of Genesis around in your mind. The garden . . . the cool of the day . . . among the trees . . . the sound of walking . . . the Lord God.

Now, imagine yourself in the garden in the cool of the day. Using the sensory description tool describe the garden through touch, taste, sight, smell, sound. Let go of the children's-picture-Bible image and see the garden paradise that is in your imagination.

What does it look like? What flowers do you see? What types of trees?

What is under your feet? Grass, moss, sand, rock?

Can you sense the air? Is it cool, humid, arid?

Take a deep breath and discover what it smells like in the garden.

Listen for the sound of God walking. Do you hear him asking, "Where are you?" How do you respond?

Protective Coating

When you imagined God asking you "Where are you?" you may have said, "Here I am!" or you may have hidden among the trees.

We are timid about drawing attention to ourselves and to our ideas. When we are rejected for our creativity, it hurts because our creativity is connected with the image of God in us. We love to create, long to create, strain to create something that expresses our soul. But the minute we step out, we know we are inviting misunderstanding and rejection.

In Genesis 3:8 we read that when the man and his wife heard God, they hid in the trees because they realized they were naked. We do the same thing. We cover our real responses and put up a good front. Being covered is not an inappropriate response; in Genesis 3:21 we read that God covers Adam and Eve with garments of skin. So the issue is not being covered; the issue is how we cover ourselves.

❑ When you are rejected, how do you respond? What happens to your body language? What is your first thought? What do you usually say or do?

Journal

❑ How do you respond when you are complimented? Think about your physical, mental and emotional reactions.

❑ We wrap ourselves in a protective coating to keep from getting hurt, but our lovely layers are ridiculously transparent, like saran wrap. That kind of protection only wraps you up tight and stops your pores from breathing. It does not keep anyone from seeing you; it only keeps them from reaching you. And worst of all, even if we build up a thick shell, we still get hurt. What metaphor can you use to describe your protective covering?

I have come that they may have life, and have it to the full.

JOHN 10:10

Have you ever held a brainstorming session with colleagues? The goal of brainstorming is to come up with a bunch of ideas and see if one appears that will appeal to everyone. The atmosphere starts out charged and excited. You and your coworkers know and accept each other. You cram around the table, pen in hand, ready to brainstorm. Then you sit there looking at each other. Finally

Tool

someone says, "Well, this probably isn't any good, but . . ."

In order to protect ourselves from rejection, we develop seemingly safe ways to process our creative ideas. Right before you offer an idea you might reach for a qualifying phrase. Finish each one of these sentences with "here's my idea," and see if one of them sounds like something you would say.

❏ I'm not creative, but . . .

❏ I'm sure you won't be interested in this, but . . .

❏ I'm not sure I understand what you are saying, but . . .

❏ I'm certain this is not right, but . . .

❏ I know this is not what you want, but . . .

❏ This is silly, but . . .

❏ I don't know anything about this, but . . .

What qualifier do you use?

Creative Blocks

You can peel off one of your protective layers when you recognize what blocks your creativity and choose not to reach for it. You can choose not to qualify your creative offering when you are secure in the protection God offers. According to God's Word, it is possible to be covered and protected while being real and available.

Explore

❏ Read Isaiah 61:1-3. How does God respond to your hurt?

❏ What would God have you wear instead of a "spirit of despair"?

❏ Look at Psalm 45:6-9, 13-15. Referring to this verse and the verse from Isaiah, describe a garment of praise and the oil of gladness.

❏ What is the difference between your protective coating and the garment God has for you?

❏ How is God planting you to display his splendor?

❏ Will you let God display his splendor in your creative life?

But thanks be to God, who always lead us in triumphal procession in Christ and through us spreads everywhere the fragrance of the knowledge of him. For we are to God the aroma of Christ among those who are being saved and those who are perishing.

2 CORINTHIANS 2:14-15

❏ Do these verses give you the confidence to offer an idea without qualifying it?

❏ Ask God to anoint you with the oil of gladness and to cover you with the garment of praise.

R.S.V.P.

When we step out creatively, we are risking misunderstanding and rejection. But God invites us to be led in a triumphal procession through life. By our offerings we can be the fragrant aroma of Christ to God and to his people.

You are covered in God's grace. Will you consider your creative life as an offering? Take a moment to breathe in the aroma around you. The scent of my life today is sticky, sweet peanut butter and jelly hands. Not exactly the aroma of perfection that wafts from the pages of *House Beautiful,* but I want to enjoy where I am right now. Let the fragrance fill your senses and remind you that to God your life is a sweet perfume.

Worship

R.S.V.P. to God's creative invitation by singing one of these hymns:

"Shield About Me"

"Oil of Gladness"

"Spirit of the Living God"

"Come, Let Us Worship and Bow Down"

Chapter 4

Creative Environment: A Safe Place for Your Imagination

> As you come to him, the living Stone—rejected by men but chosen by God and precious to him—you also, like living stones, are being built into a spiritual house to be a holy priesthood, offering spiritual sacrifices acceptable to God through Jesus Christ.
>
> *1 PETER 2:4-5*

*I*F SOMEONE INVITED ME TO A CREATIVITY PARTY, I would feel tremendous pressure to bring a finished piece that displayed my creative essence—a brilliant, innovative finished piece. (That is, I'd want it to be better than what anyone else is bringing!)

When God invites us to creativity, he invites us to be available to him. Isn't that a great kind of invitation? It is different from the demands we place on ourselves. We are invited to partake of his divine nature, to participate in his divine plan and to offer to him our spiritual sacrifices. We have been invited to use our imagination and our creativity, and the only gift we need to bring is our readiness.

Let's get ready for the party by developing an environment conducive to consecrated creativity. We need good soil so our roots can go deep into the warm ground. Then we will be able to reach more easily up to the heavens and out to others.

Seeds and Circumstances

Explore

❏ Read Mark 4:3-9, 13-20. What is the seed that Jesus tells about?

❏ What happens to the seed on the path?

❏ What does the seed sown on the rocky place lack?

❏ What causes people who are like that seed to fall away?

❏ To what three circumstances are thorns or weeds likened in verse 19?

❏ When the plants are choked by the weeds, what results?

❏ What do the seeds that are sown on good soil produce?

❏ What process do the seeds go through so that they will be productive?

❏ Which seed do you relate to most and why?

When I started performing a show at a theme park, I was angry and desperate. I wanted to be an actor, a star of the stage, and I had been traveling with my comedy troupe in the hopes of making enough money to move to a theater town like Chicago or Seattle. When the comedy work dried up, I lobbied hard to get the job at the theme park, but I was angry about the redirection of my career.

The show was a fun look at how to make a TV program. Upon entering, the audience members were named "Executive Producers" and would move through four different rooms meeting one of the characters that made their TV show in each room.

One day when I was several years into my contract, I was waiting to go on stage. My audience was in the first room with Stan, the actor doing the pre-show. As soon as Stan's five-minute show was over, he would send the audience into my room, where for five minutes I would demonstrate, in a slightly comedic way, how to edit a television show. Because each show was only five minutes long, we each did thirteen of them a day. Thirteen shows a day, five days a week for three years. Hardly the glamorous, standing-ovation, flowers-in-the-dressing-room life I had been looking for.

While I waited for Stan to finish and send the group to me, I picked up something to read. The pages flopped open, and there staring at me from the pages of *American Theater* magazine was Nancy Hower, a college friend of mine. We had done plays together, competed for roles, worked in the shop tearing apart fake chimneys. And now here she was doing a play in Manhattan. My mouth went dry.

"Well, look at this!" I said a little too loudly to my friend Joel. "It's my old college buddy doing a play off-Broadway."

"And you are about to do the Edit Show!" he said, laughing.

"Yes, I am!" I started laughing. I picked up my microphone; Stan was almost done. I was laughing harder now.

Joel came over and grabbed hold of my shoulders to hold

me up. "Maybe Tommy Tune will be in this crowd and discover you," he teased, trying to put me in a better mood. But as soon as he said that, I started to cry, as loudly and as hysterically as I had been laughing. Tommy Tune would not be in the audience, only two hundred tourists from Michigan with newly pink legs and big floppy sun hats.

"Can you do this?" Joel asked.

"Sure, of course. Nancy is where she is supposed to be, and this is where I am supposed to be." This realization provoked a new wave of hysteria from me.

The doors were opening and the audience was entering. Joel patted my back as he took the microphone from me and pushed me backstage.

I was in the right place. My time in theme-park entertainment birthed many good things. I had started writing sketches for church, practicing a form I had learned by doing thirteen five-minute shows a day. And my perspective on my work did change while I was there. By the time I left nine years later, my work was no longer about me and my performance but about serving the audience. That attitude has carried me into ministry.

If I had developed a good creative environment would I have cried when I saw Nancy's picture? No doubt I would have. But if I had not been so choked by the weeds of ambition, I think I would have stopped crying and gotten it together enough to perform my role.

Three years after seeing Nancy's picture, I was flipping through TV channels while nursing my newborn son, and there was Nancy Hower, one of the new Star Trek cast members, giving birth to an alien baby. I laughed and cried for joy. Instead of feeling separated and forgotten, I felt a kinship; Nancy was in Los Angeles getting work as the mother of an alien, and I was in my Florida loft holding my son.

 Journal

❑ What elements in your environment or your circumstances contribute to your creative life?

❑ What detracts from your creativity?

❑ What do you struggle with in your current situation?

❑ What might God be using in your life to strengthen the connection between you and your creativity?

❑ When your creativity is strengthened, what is the impact on your relationship with God?

Good Soil

"Prone to wander, Lord, I feel it, prone to leave the God I love." These words from "Come, Thou Fount of Every Blessing" express how I feel when my focus goes to how other people are doing. When my eyes are fixed on my circumstances, my path becomes rocky, and I feel the weeds of ambition around my throat.

I've had friends who started out knowing Jesus but fell away from him. Now they live in a strange existence in which they know the truth but have to work to keep distant from it. It is heartbreaking and scary to think that my sin could lead me to make Jesus my "ex." I fervently pray for good soil.

Experience

Use Mark 4:20 as an outline to help you develop a prayer for good soil. Increase the soil's texture by adding specific promises that God makes to you in his Word. If you are not sure that God has given you a promise before, then fill in your prayer with one of Paul's prayers from Colossians 1:9-14 or Ephesians 3:14-21. When we pray God's Word, our feet become rooted in the best soil, his eternal plan.

Here are some examples to get you started.

Lord give me good soil:

❏ nurturing "the faith and love that spring from the hope that is stored up for you in heaven" (Colossians 1:5)

Cause me to hear the Word:

❏ understanding "the word of truth, the gospel" (Colossians 1:5)

❏ "lifting me out of the slimy pit . . . he set my feet on a rock" (Psalm 40:2)

❏ "knowing your will through all spiritual wisdom and understanding" (Colossians 1:9)

Cause me to accept the Word:

❏ growing since the day I heard it (Colossians 1:6)

❏ grasping "how wide and long and high and deep is the love of Christ" (Ephesians 3:18)

Cause me to produce a crop:

❏ "bearing fruit in every good work" (Colossians 1:10)

❏ accomplishing "more than all we ask or imagine" (Ephesians 3:20)

Boundaries

One summer I went to New York to study acting and had the great privilege of taking a musical theater class from Elizabeth Parrish. I had never understood the phrase *joie de vivre* until I saw it embodied in Miss Parrish; she was electric, joyful and spicy. Every moment was valuable to her. She must have been at least fifty, and during the day she taught and at night she was on Broadway as Jacqueline in *La Cage*. Most actors get tired and bored doing a show eight times a week with the usual Broadway contract of nine months. She had been playing her part for three years and had never missed a performance. Before playing Jacqueline in *La Cage*, she had been Helga Ten Dorp in *Deathtrap* for five years. There is no one else like her.

On my first day in Elizabeth's class I was to go through the steps of auditioning for a musical. I did this exactly as I had done it at several auditions. It works like this: When you audition for a musical, you appear on a bare stage in a white spotlight. Sitting in the dark are the director, the producer, the casting director, the costumer and any number of other people. Near the edge of the stage is a piano and an accompanist. In every other acting class I had taken, I had been instructed to carry my sheet music in and hand it quickly to the pianist, to head straight to the light and to bow my head. When I was ready to sing, I was to nod, and the music would start.

Elizabeth stopped me only one line into my song. "Look at you, you are shaking!" she said. "Your emotions and nerves are overwhelming you because you do not own this space. You are swimming in a vast ocean. Come into this room again and make it your backyard wading pool. Possess the talent, do not let it possess you."

I tried again. I came through the door, greeted the pianist and asked his name. I touched the piano and felt its wood under my fingers. I looked at the walls and felt the floor under my feet as I walked toward the pool of light. Lifting my face, I could feel the spotlight's heat on my forehead. I took a deep breath, looked at the pianist and said, "I'm ready, Glenn." He played and I sang.

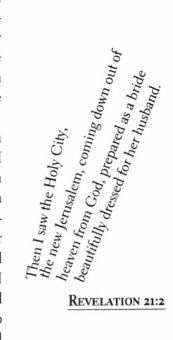

Then I saw the Holy City, the new Jerusalem, coming down out of heaven from God, prepared as a bride beautifully dressed for her husband.

REVELATION 21:2

O afflicted city lashed by storms and not comforted,
I will build you with stones of turquoise,
your foundations with sapphires.
I will make your battlements of rubies,
your gates of sparkling jewels,
and all your walls of precious stones.

ISAIAH 54:11-12

You may become overwhelmed by your fears, your emotions and your passion for your ideas. Your surroundings, your environment, your boundaries are there to help you. Use your boundaries to shape your creativity. Have dominion over your imagination; don't let it have dominion over you.

A city is a great metaphor for your creative environment because cities are defined not only by boundaries, but by what happens in them.

Often I try to be a holy city by being very moral or by knowing a lot about the Bible or by cultivating a good image. But there is a difference between a moral city and a holy city. A moral city has very high walls, and the people inside work very hard at being good and at keeping the bad people out. In a holy city you focus on God, who sets your city on a hill and pours light through the walls that he has built of precious stones. Some people are drawn to the holy city, some run away from it, and others throw rocks at it. But inside the city you are living out a holy life. In your city unique and creative ideas flow freely and are enjoyed as a generous expression of God.

Journal

❏ What metaphor can you use to illustrate trusting God with your imagination?

❏ What do you see when you picture your ideas and expressions coming from a safe and beautiful place?

❏ What kind of haven, large or small, is God giving you for your creativity right now?

Building a City

If the roots of your creative life are in Christ, then you are safe to experience the farthest reaches of your imagination. It is not necessary to share every idea with others; some ideas are just for you. Good soil provides a playground for you and God. Appropriate boundaries provide a city within which to work out ideas. In Matthew 5:14 we read that Jesus says that we are a city on a hill. When we have fertile soil and a protected environment, failure can bring redirection, not destruction. Rejection need not cause us to build higher, denser walls; instead, it can shape the ways in which we do what God has given us to do.

Imagine

"You are the light of the world. A city on a hill cannot be hidden." (Matthew 5:14)

Close your eyes and take a deep breath. Settle into your chair and think about Matthew 5:14.

Imagine your life as a city. Picture how God has built its wall and its gate. What does the city look like? Is it a bustling metropolis or a quiet town, a country village? What kind of buildings are in your city? Businesses, a library, restaurants? Perhaps the city is a suburb with many houses. Describe the city with all your senses: Where is the city located? The Scottish highlands, a tropical island, Iowa? Where is the church located? What does it look like? What activities go on in the city? Do you like it there? How do the other people in the city respond to you? What is your activity in the city? In what part of town do you feel most comfortable?

God is expansive, but he's made us limited creatures. We are limited by geography, age, generation, gender, abilities, experiences and the list goes on. Some people would say, "No, no, you're not limited." But really we are.

LORD, you have assigned me
   my portion and my cup;
   you have made my lot
      secure.
The boundary lines have
   fallen for me in pleasant
   places;
   surely I have a delightful
   inheritance.

PSALM 16:5-6

Most of us consider limits something to rebel against, something to be exceeded or stretched. But God is stretching us. Within the boundaries of our lives we can experience God's abundance. He is always going beyond our limitations to achieve eternal purposes. This is what God does in you: he tells you who you are, and then he pours out his grace and makes you more than you are, more than you ever could be. He makes you like Jesus.

In-House Retreat

We recently downsized. We sold our house and moved into an apartment. I love it! I was so happy to get rid of the clutter. There was a sacrifice, though. Our apartment does not have a porch. Every book about writing tells you to have a writing room, and my porch was my creative spot. I kept all my journals out there, several good pens and some books that inspire me. On the walls were a wreath with the flowers from our wedding and a picture someone drew for my birthday. There was no clock or phone on the porch. I felt comfortable and inspired there.

Even though I don't have a specific room anymore, I know how important the right environment is for creative thinking. So I got a special coffee cup. It is really big and has colors that inspire me. Now when I want to spend some time mulling over ideas, I get out my cup and make a pot of tea or coffee, and wherever I end up becomes my "porch."

Experience

Make a safe haven for creative thought. Use a chair, room, porch, corner, cup or picture—whatever will help you to relax and remember that you are safe to explore your imagination. Let your safe haven remind you that you need to spend time connecting with God in order to experience your creative life.

Worship

Sit in your safe haven and worship the Lord with one of these hymns:
"Be Thou My Vision"
"Come, Thou Fount of Every Blessing"
"For the Beauty of the Earth"
"Leaning on the Everlasting Arms"

Chapter 5

Creative Expansion: Beyond the Borders

Enlarge the place of your tent,

>stretch your tent curtains wide,

>do not hold back;

lengthen you cords,

>strengthen your stakes.

ISAIAH 54:2

*A*T THE SMALL LIBERAL ARTS COLLEGE I ATTENDED, Sister Kate used to say that when freshmen declare theater as their major, they are declaring themselves late to class for the next four years. And she was right; I admit it! I used the label "creative artist" to excuse myself from responsibility. We label people creative, then grant them immunity from being like the rest of us. We put them in a special category.

God does not treat his artistry with such a cavalier attitude. He takes care of the details and claims sovereignty over the outcome. What that means to your creative life is that unearthing your creativity does not grant you immunity from doing the dishes. Sorry. But the good news is that your creativity includes everything in your life, not just the artistic projects on your wish list.

"Some artists look at the world around them and see chaos, and instead of discovering cosmos, they reproduce chaos, on canvas, in music, in words. As far as I can see, the reproduction of chaos is neither art nor is it Christian."

MADELEINE L'ENGLE,
WALKING ON WATER

In chapter four we talked about our limitations, and we established a home for creativity within those limitations. In

Spring Water

Psalm 16:5 we learn that those boundaries, our portion and cup, are assigned by God and that the boundary lines are pleasant. It is from within your safe haven that God expands you. This is completely different from the way in which I try to expand my life. I usually decide that what I have to offer is no good anymore. I fret about needing to learn something new and be something different. Sure, I am an actor, but what I really need to be is a singer, even though no one is asking me to sing and I don't enjoy the discipline of music. I decide that I must grow. I take lessons, join the choir, quickly become frustrated with my lack of ability and quit.

That is not how God expands you. First of all, he does not discard your natural inclinations. He made you. He likes you. He wants to use your abilities for his glory. God does not start over with you; he redeems you.

In this chapter we will discover that the cup God has assigned to us truly does overflow.

Explore

❏ Read John 4:7-30, 39-42. Look at the Samaritan woman's words. What did she know about herself?

❏ What did she know about her heritage?

about her faith?

about her role?

❑ Now look at Jesus' response to the Samaritan woman. What did he know about her?

❑ What did he know about her circumstances?

about her needs?

about her faith?

JOHN 10:14

❑ In what verses do we read that Jesus pinpoints who the Samaritan woman is?

❑ What does he offer to the woman?

❑ What does Jesus say will happen to the well water?

❑ Where will the water that Jesus gives come from?

❏ What are the effects of the water that Jesus gives?

❏ How does Jesus expand the Samaritan woman's thinking?

Jesus does not offer an external change of behavior. He knows you specifically and calls you by name. He offers living water that springs up from inside you! When Jesus expands you, he begins with who you are at your core, then changes you incrementally. He moves you beyond your limitations and expectations.

Being creative does not require you to step out of your life and into an artistic activity. You can start with what you know about yourself and then watch how Jesus expands you.

Journal

❏ What do you know about your heritage?

about your role?

about your faith?

❏ What do you like about your creativity?

❏ What were your dreams when you were a kid?

What are they now?

❏ What has Jesus said about you?

"There is a vitality, a life force, an energy, a quickening, that is translated through you into action, and because there is only one of you in all time, this expression is unique. And if you block it, it will never exist through any other medium and will be lost."

MARTHA GRAHAM

The Creative Process

I visited my son's school, and when his teacher showed me a chart she made for him I burst into tears. She had the numbers one to twenty-five across the top. Underneath there were schools of tiny fish that she had drawn, cut out, and laminated. Henry was to count the fish and put them under the appropriate number. I was overcome by how her creativity was serving my son; not only would I not have come up with that idea, I could not have executed it that well. While I dabbed my eyes, she looked at me with that "but you're the creative one" expression.

We have expectations of people we consider creative. We think of creative types as fun, vibrant and easy going. On the other hand, we expect them to be flighty, lost in their own world, a bit outrageous. In the introduction we considered our image of "the perfect Christian." Now let's take a look at what "the creative type" conjures up.

Go ahead, describe the creative type:

The creative type of person that I aspire to be has her hair pulled back and kept loosely in place with a pencil or whatever is handy. Her flowing peasant blouse does not necessarily match her brightly patterned skirt. She has on big jewelry, more "art festival" than "Target," and she always wears sandals. My friend Stacy looks like this. I equate her sparkling eyes and easy manner with her talents as a poet, a mother and a friend. And I consider my creative life either greater than or less than hers based on which one of us looks most like my image of the creative type each day. The really silly thing is that another friend, Lynn, judges her creative life by how much she looks or behaves like me.

We separate ourselves from the creative life by thinking that being artsy is the only valuable creative expression. It's a good way out; heaven knows there is always someone more artsy than I am. But artistic expression and creative expression are not the same thing because creativity does not always result in a work of art. If you figured out a way to potty train your resistant toddler, it wasn't artistic, but it was creative.

Journal

❏ What everyday activities require creativity from you?

❏ What comes naturally to you in your work?

❏ What comes naturally to you in your home life?

❏ In your relationships?

❏ How do you feel when your originality and your everyday world collide?

We are intimidated by creativity when we honor only one of its aspects, but there are two components to the creative process: the creative and the productive. Experts say that the two phases can take various forms: for example, either writing or editing, either rehearsing or performing, either exercising the creative spirit or exercising the critical spirit. These dichotomies can reinforce the idea that one part is creative and the other not. But the creative process involves both the original idea and its practical execution.

In his excellent book *Whack on the Side of the Head: How You Can Be More Creative*, Roger Van Oech describes the two parts of the creative process as soft thinking and hard thinking. His approach esteems both aspects. In the creative life, creativity is not a separate act but an integral part of being. In our personalities we are not limited by the separation of the creative phase and the productive phase. It just feels that way because we have decided that artists belong in the first phase and the rest of us belong in the second. We are convinced that productivity is not creativity, that productivity is boring.

We will expand our lives so that we can be both creative and productive at the same time, but first let's stay in these separate modes for a while. There are cases in which the creative process must be separated into two phases, in a brainstorming situation, for example. Test the two phases: have a family meeting (even a family of one can do this) to consider where to go on vacation. Let everyone throw out ideas without worrying about their practicality. Your goal is to get as many ideas on the page as possible.

"Where do you want to go on vacation?"
❏ The Cannes film festival

❏ The beach
❏ The mountains
❏ Fishing
❏ A cruise of the Greek isles
❏ Home under the covers
❏ The library
❏ The in-laws
❏ London
❏ The Grand Canyon
❏ Hawaii
❏ Next door

That is the idea-churning portion of the process. Now you enter the productive phase. You research how much it would cost to go to Hawaii. You find out what would need to happen for you to visit London or the Grand Canyon. Once you've gathered your information, you can make a decision.

What happens to you during the brainstorming process? Do you squirm in your seat when people throw out ideas, unable to stop yourself from thinking, "That one won't work. Who wants to go on a cruise?" Or do you relish the inventive part, coming up with a million ideas, then duck your head when someone asks, "Who will get this one started for us?"

What are your natural creative inclinations? Like the woman at the well, pinpoint where you are before you try to expand. Here is a new tool, the word jam, to help you to investigate how God has wired you.

Tool

When you are dealing with a huge concept, it helps to break it into manageable bits. You can't touch a concept like creative inclinations. It's like a huge, four-layer chocolate cake that looks too delicious to cut into. But if the cake was presented already sliced and on Styrofoam plates, you would pick up a plastic fork and delight in your piece. And if you felt like it you could have another, the corner one, then maybe that small one with the extra icing, and that other one over on the end table. All right, let's stop thinking about four-layer chocolate cake.

The process of discovering your creative inclinations is much too big, but the word-jam tool breaks big ideas into bite-size pieces.

In the last ten years I have been working on material about creativity one-on-one, in small groups and in training seminars, but when it came time to write the material in book form, I froze up. Write a book on creativity and Christ? Can't be done. Where would I begin?

I started with a word jam to see if I had any feelings on creativity. Here's what was swimming in my heart and mind:

Creativity and Christ Word Jam
Alice's Journal, February 27, 1999

richness	surprise!	Looking	texture	contrary	listening
different	developing	obtuse	bizarre	discerning	wacky
out-there	inspired	offered	unreal	creative	breathed
beyond	inventive	delightful	lending	speaking	finger-paints
washed	linear	squiggly	aglow	kaleidoscope	uniform
weaving	cuneiform	harp	interacting	jaundiced	twang
vibrant	set apart	set aside	savoring	delicious	constant
moving	free straining	Play-doh	perceiving	pining	delicate
persevering	piercing	receiving			

That is one way to use word jam: start with an original word or phrase and list various words under it. Don't worry; you are not a thesaurus or a dictionary, and this is not a test. You do not have to be correct. Let a flow of words come out, and see what happens. If *creative* means cuneiform to you, just let it. Do not evaluate your thinking at this point. Just pick up a pen and scribble down words that relate to you in this moment. Do not spend more than three minutes on creating each list.

Word jam on the following two words. Set your watch for three minutes. Go!

Creative:

Okay, set your watch for another three minutes. Go!
Productive:

Another way to use this exercise is to fill in the blanks.
Finish a sentence on your theme. Just words, not explana-
tions. Pick up a pen. No more than three minutes. Go!
❑ Being creative means . . .

❑ Being productive means . . .

❑ Having an idea means . . .

❑ Taking an action means . . .

Now circle the words on your lists that describe you. Remember, do not try to determine which set of words is better
than the others. Both creativity and productivity are vital to
the creative process. Chances are that you will not esteem
your own process. Let that go and just be descriptive. Circle
words you relate to, then journal on the following questions.
Take your time.

❏ In which phase, the creative or the productive, do you feel most comfortable?

❏ Who in your life belongs to the opposite phase?

❏ What are your creative strengths?

❏ What are your productive strengths?

❏ Who are your creative friends, and who are your productive friends? What do you gain from each?

I like things to be very linear: explained, outlined, structured. Because of my approach I sometimes feel like an outsider in artistic circles. That is probably why my image of the creative type is Miss Free Spirit. It's also why I surround myself with people like Stacy and my husband and my best friend Clare. They love to churn out ideas, while I love to put them into action. It is easy to forget that we should not label people as creative or not creative. In the creative phase, you are acting on your ideas by being brave enough to vocalize them or to write them down. In the productive phase you are affected by ideas as you try to find the best way to achieve a goal.

The creative life relies on both phases at the same time. The two parts of the process are not separated, but flow evenly. When you are in the middle of taking an action, you may come up with an idea that will lead to completion of the project or to a new action or to another idea. And while you are pondering ideas, you may suddenly start doing. The possibilities are endless.

So let's *expand*. Stop thinking of yourself as creative or productive. If you did not think of yourself as one or the other before reading this chapter, don't start now. Instead, think about your creative life as something that is full of ideas and actions. Be aware of your strengths and rely on others when needed. Borrow from both phases when you need to, but do not say "I am not creative" or "I am not productive." Instead say, "I have a creative life. It is full of ideas and actions." Then look for opportunities to come up with ideas and take action.

Specific and Unique

God made you with specific details and unique abilities. Your personality, abilities, desires, interests and work are all opportunities to reveal facets of his character.

We are resisting the Artist's work when we try to be something that we are not. It is much better to acknowledge who we are and to participate in his process. Then we will be expanded in ways that glorify him and enrich ourselves.

Explore

❏ Let's look at Proverbs 31:10-31, where we learn about a woman who serves God with all that she is. What kind of character does the woman have?

❏ What does her character produce in the people around her?

❏ Who makes up the woman's support team?

❏ When the woman makes a profit, what does she do with it?

❏ How does the woman care for herself?

❏ How does she care for her family?

for her servants?

❏ What is the woman's attitude toward life?

❏ Why is the woman is beautiful?

❏ What do you think is the source of her strength and her wisdom?

❏ From verse 31 what do you think is the woman's reward

(see also Proverbs 12:14)?

Source of Strength

Hallelujah!
  For our Lord God
    Almighty reigns.
Let us rejoice and be glad
  and give him glory!
For the wedding of the Lamb
    has come,
  and his bride has made
    herself ready.

REVELATION 19:6-7

Of course, the one who lived the most "expanded" life on earth was the Lord Jesus. His divinity was contained in his humanity. We look at the Proverbs 31 character because she is a good example, a picture of humanity and frailty reliant on the divine. Jesus is more than just an example to look at and try to follow; he is the source of inspiration and the fulfillment of abundant living. And as his church, his body, you and I are described as his bride. With that in mind, Proverbs 31 becomes an excellent example of the kind of character God would develop in each one of us as he prepares us for union with our King.

Journal

❏ How do you see your character being moved beyond your expectations of yourself?

❏ What experiences and relationships have contributed to your growth (expansion)?

❏ How does reading about someone of godly character make you feel about God's work in preparing you for eternal life with him?

❏ If God asked the writer of Proverbs to describe your character, what would God have him write?

Close your eyes and calm your spirit. Breathe deeply and imagine God's view of your life. Put yourself in the words of Proverbs 31. Picture yourself before dawn.

Imagine

Where are you? In your kitchen, your office, your yard?

What are you wearing that displays confidence and readiness?

What does the world sound like before dawn? What does it smell like? feel like? look like?

Who is rising up and calling you blessed?

Who or what is the godly heritage you leave for the future?

Who makes up your support team? What are they doing to help you? How are you receiving their help?

Look around at your environment. Are you comfortable in it?

How does your environment cause the Lord, your spouse and your work partners to be "respected at the city gate" (Proverbs 31:23)?

What is the beauty that God sees in you?

The Proverbs 31 woman was living an expanded life because in some areas she had a natural gift or ability, and in other areas her qualities were learned by experience and in relationship with others. Both her gifts and her skills were infused by the Holy Spirit, producing eternal results in her and others. Her amazing character comes from her reliance on God, who fills her with the Holy Spirit. She was available to

Creative Commitment

There are different kinds of gifts, but the same Spirit. There are different kinds of service, but the same Lord. There are different kinds of working, but the same God works all of them in all men. Now to each one the manifestation of the Spirit is given for the common good.

1 Corinthians 12:4-7

new thoughts that led to expression and action. Her kind of life is attainable only through the grace and power that God has given us in accordance with our faith. Having godly character is not about achieving but about receiving.

Think back to the creative and productive phases you listed in the journal activity on page 72 and which phase you feel most comfortable in.

I wonder, *Does the fact that I like structure make me boring? Is my linear thinking stifling my creativity?* No, I dig deep and think full thoughts. I do not write with colored pens or wear three different earrings, but I am creative. I am free to think and feel and dream. It is okay to be me, creative in my straightness and within my boundaries. And why not? A limitless fount of ideas flows from God's throne. So does my structured creative life invalidate my friend Stacy's creativity found in poems and flowing shirts and tender mothering? No. Her wispy responsive, wellspring of ideas can produce fruit. When she needs to move on ideas, God's power can move in her, calling her to the obedience of creating cosmos from chaos. Then he can expand her dreams and motivate her to produce them. He does that in you too.

Your creative process is valuable. Your inclinations are designed by God for his purposes and fulfilled by him for his glory. If you are linear, like me, be expanded, remembering that ideas are the warp and woof in the weave of your actions. If your creativity is "in the moment," look for moments of action and take tiny steps toward realizing your ideas. Look at the people around you and draw deeply from their strengths in the creative and productive phases. Offer them your creative life as well.

Experience

Do you still feel stuck or tempted to say that you're not creative? Or do you have tons of ideas but you are unsure about acting on them? Try this. Word jam on these sentences:

To experience my "creative side" I will . . .

Alice's Journal
May 15, 2000

To enjoy my idea phase I will
❏ learn to receive
❏ take deep breaths
❏ embrace that little
   moment before I act
❏ stop being afraid of
   awkward pauses
❏ ask Stacy to affirm me
❏ ask God if I am creative

To take action and produce what I have an idea about I will . . .

To balance my action phase I will
❏ stop taking charge just
   because I'm in the room
❏ give my new idea to
   another person
❏ listen for my cue to act
❏ write down my ideas in a
   journal
❏ take a walk
❏ ask God if he values my idea

Commit to being available to ideas and actions. Make them small. Make them possible. Rely on your source of strength.

Worship God for being the source.
Sing "Immortal, Invisible" or "Jesus Loves Me."
Now lean on Jesus by meditating on the following verses. Imagine Jesus giving you water, streams of water, living water that flows from within you.

Worship

> On the last and greatest day of the Feast, Jesus stood and said in a loud voice, "If anyone is thirsty, let him come to me and drink. Whoever believes in me, as the Scripture has said, streams of living water will flow from within him." (John 7:37-38)

When you feel like your creativity is not being valued by those around you, lean on the following passage. Think about his strength and your weariness. Replace *Jacob* and *Israel* with your name. Listen for God's voice. Is there a gentle laugh wooing you back to his strength or a strong reprimand reminding you to get back in the yard before you get hurt?

> Why do you say, O Jacob,
>   and complain, O Israel,
> "My way is hidden from the LORD;
>   My cause is disregarded by my God"?
> Do you not know?
>   Have you not heard?
> The LORD is the everlasting God,
>   the Creator of the ends of the earth.
> He will not grow tired or weary,
>   and his understanding no one can fathom.
> He gives strength to the weary
>   and increases the power of the weak. (Isaiah 40:27-29)

Chapter 6

Creative Calling: Responding to the Hand of God

> The creation waits in eager expectation for the sons of God to
> be revealed.... And we know that in all things God works for
> the good of those who love him, who have been called accord-
> ing to his purpose.
>
> ROMANS 8:19, 28

*A*LL OF CREATION EAGERLY ANTICIPATES YOUR BE-
ing brought fully into the glorious reality of Christ; the
whole universe waits for your debut! How exciting is that?
Are you eagerly expecting abundance? Well, maybe.

So far during our excursion we looked at fears of being
different, being hurt, being rejected, taking risks. Now we
need to go to the other end of the spectrum and explore
our fear of success. God is expanding us, and that can be
more disconcerting than failing.

Abundance is more frightening than failure because we
are used to failure and well acquainted with disappoint-
ment. If there is no picture in our mind for abundant, creative living, we would rather stay in our timid world.

Creative thinking produces fear because it is wild, it
changes us, it leads us in new directions, and it reveals the
inner working of our hearts. It is threatening. Sometimes
when dictators come to power they imprison or kill the ac-

Holy Danger

tors, the writers and the poets because artists challenge people's thinking. But God is not a dictator. He wants you to have wild, dangerous, exciting, outrageous, creative thoughts. If he didn't, he wouldn't dare allow something as explosive as his Word to live in your heart. He wants your thought life to be challenged because, my friend, you and I are the dictators; we are the ones crushing and imprisoning the Holy Spirit.

Sound extreme? Let me give you an example. One Sunday my pastor asked me to lead the worship team in prayer for the service. As I prayed for them, I had an image of God drawing some friends of mine to that service. Did I weave that into my prayer? "Oh, Lord, draw the unchurched, the unsaved, even now, draw my friends to this service." Nope, instead I said to that little voice inside of me, "Hush. I'm trying to pray. Besides, the service is going to start in a few minutes and my friends could never make it in time."

Now in that story, who had the wild, exciting thought, and who was the dictator? You can't see me, but my hand is raised.

Our creative life is not a path of recklessness. We have received the Spirit of Jesus, the living Lord, and when we ask him, he will gladly lead us into all truth.

> If any of you lacks wisdom,
> he should ask God,
> who gives generously to all
> without finding fault,
> and it will be given to him.
>
> JAMES 1:5

Explore

❑ Read 1 Corinthians 2:6-16. From this passage what can we expect will happen to the wisdom of this age?

❑ How are the plans of God revealed to us?

❑ How does the Spirit know God's plans?

❏ According to these verses, how do we understand life and exercise discernment?

The Spirit moves in us, giving us the mind of Christ that feeds our creative life. This abundance is scary; it is deeper than we can imagine. What would we do if we were experiencing God continually, available in every minute to use our abilities fully for him? It is too much for our little selves to handle. So don't handle it. Do the thing God has put in front of you. Start there and be fully available to the new thing he will accomplish as you do it.

> Now to him who is able to do immeasurably more than all we ask or imagine, according to his power at work within us, to him be glory in the church and in Christ Jesus throughout all generations for ever and ever! Amen.
>
> Ephesians 3:20

❏ List the interesting and inventive ideas you had this week.

Journal

❏ List the fears that went along with those ideas.

❏ What did you do with your ideas?

❏ What does having the mind of Christ mean to you?

Acting on the things in front of us is hard only when we start to second guess whether we will succeed. When we

Heeding the Call

take our eyes off Jesus and put them on our ability to bring about an outcome, we lose the motivation to act, to walk or to try. But we can let the Spirit propel us forward in the small and grand things he is giving us to do, and leave the success and failure to him. He will bring glory to himself through it all.

Explore

❏ Read Exodus 35:30—36:2. What abilities did Bezalel and Oholiab have?

❏ What kind of work were they to do?

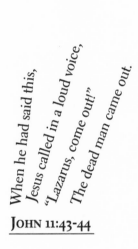

When he had said this, Jesus called in a loud voice, "Lazarus, come out!" The dead man came out.

JOHN 11:43-44

❏ Picture them at work. What thoughts, feelings and attitudes would they have had?

❏ Do you think they had these abilities before the time that we are reading about? Why or why not?

❏ What is the difference between skill, ability and knowledge?

❏ What sets Bezalel's and Oholiab's creative abilities apart according to Exodus 35:31?

❑ What do you think Bezalel and Oholiab experienced by being willing to do the work?

❑ What new thing is God calling you to do that requires creativity?

Journal

❑ What old thing has God called you to do that also requires creativity?

❑ What natural abilities has God given you?

❑ What skills has he called you to learn through the years?

❑ What knowledge is he giving you?

❑ How are those abilities, skills and knowledge enabling you to live a creative life?

You are being called to creative living. Your very nature is creative, and as Jesus reigns in your heart he purifies that nature. Start keeping a log during the day. Notice when you do something creative and mark down when you have a new thought or are available to an inventive idea. You will be surprised at the extent to which creativity is a part of your everyday life.

Observing and Expressing

The goal is to live creatively, not to experience individual creative events. Resist the pressure to create something artistic and perfect in order to prove yourself creatively. The goal of a creative life is expression, not perfection; you have the freedom to pour out your heart to God, regardless of how well you do it.

That said, we need skills for creative living. Skills are very important to a true artist. Technique is the channel for the imagination; without it the expression is unclear. The basics of technique are easier to grasp than they sound: to paint you need to know how to hold a brush; to write a sonnet you need to know how many beats are in a line. Singing soprano requires the disciplines of breathing properly and reading music.

The artistry of the creative life is in seeing what God is doing and being available to reveal his working. This requires the techniques of observing and expressing.

Explore

❏ Read John 2:1-11. Why do you think Mary went to Jesus when the wine was gone?

❏ In verse 4 we read that Jesus respectfully reminds Mary that his time has not yet come. How does Mary respond to Jesus?

❑ Look at the steps Jesus asked the servants to take. What would their thoughts and feelings have been as they went through this process?

❑ In verse 11 what do we read was the result of the miracle?

Mary and the servants at the Cana wedding were watching and ready. They looked to Jesus and responded to only him. How easy it would have been for Mary to pout when her son implied he was no longer accountable to her, only to his Father. Instead she takes an attitude of readiness. You can feel the electricity and anticipation in her words: "Do whatever he tells you."

Likewise the servants could have copped an attitude: "We need wine, not water. Can you believe this guy? Filling those urns with water will take way too long and they will be too heavy. What's the point of this?" Instead, we have the powerful and compact statement: "They did so." Additionally, they do not correct the master of the banquet or make an announcement or point to Jesus. They saw, they knew, they acted, and God says that Jesus' glory was revealed.

❑ How are you seeing God working in your life?

Journal

❑ How are you available to his glory being revealed in and through the role you have now?

❏ Do you feel you need to change roles for God to be glorified? Why?

Trampling out the Whine

**Alice's Journal,
February 6, 1999**

10 reasons I would want to be pregnant:
1. to hold a newborn
2. to prove everyone wrong
3. to have a sister for Henry
4. so I wouldn't have to work as a performer anymore
5. so I could buy a new wardrobe
6. to see how big God is
7. to fulfill God's will for my family
8. because I don't want to adopt
9. to have a big family when I'm old
10. because I'd love it

I have to confess that I have a problem with journal writing. If I sit down to write and I have no direction, all I do is whine. When I told my writing teacher why I hated journaling, he said, "Yes, but in a journal, I'm very pro whine."

Fine. I got out my journal and tried to burn through the whine with the idea that once I got the whining done I would be free to hear from God. It didn't seem to work. I wallowed. "Besides," I wrote, "I don't want to write about my feelings! They are such bad barometers for me. They are not truth! I want truth! I don't care that much about my feelings."

That's when I realized that even though I may not care about my feelings, God does. He is interested because my feelings are a good barometer for how I am responding to his truth. Again I determined that I would journal, but to keep from wallowing, I decided to use a writing technique called timed journaling. For fifteen minutes a day I would write on a theme without editing as I went along. This time I took my journal to work so I could write about my observations on the show I was performing. The only boundaries I set were fifteen minutes and no whining. We had a great show and I could hardly wait to pick up my pen and start writing. But when I began, I found myself listing reasons why I should have another baby! Who knew that was what was on my heart? Not me. The list was awful, icky, poorly constructed, but once I had it on paper, I was able to talk freely with God about my feelings on the subject.

During the next session I wanted to journal on the upcoming sermon topic. Instead I wrote a terrible free-verse poem about my son. The poem feels sweet and tender.

Even though my expression was not on the chosen topic, my commitment to observe and express was causing me to experience deep emotion in a creative way. By being available to observe God's working and to turn it into expression, I freed up my journaling. I was not whining or wallowing. I was not trying to produce something great. I was communing with my Lord and hearing from him as I put words on paper.

It is not necessary to keep a specific journal format when you write. You may write a list, a poem, a Dear Diary letter, an outline, whatever. Just by picking up a pen you will heighten your ability to see and respond.

Take fifteen minutes. Pick up a pen and start writing. Do not cross out any words; do not go back and rewrite. Just write. If you need a topic, pick one of these:

❏ things you love to do that you consider creative
❏ things you are terrified of doing that you consider creative
❏ things you do in your daily life that you have never considered creative

Pick up your pen for fifteen minutes and see what happens.

Experience

**Alice's Journal,
February 8, 1999**

HB
I hear him now, rattling away in his room.
　The softest, most needy, tearful, fearful boy.
　Who is the most confident, laughing, zesty, bright, teasing, independent boy.

He comes to the door shaken, looking for me. Needing me.
　He reminds me of Mt. St. Helen's.
　Ice cream cone topped sweetness, glorious beauty. Packing the wallop of 50,000 tons of dynamite, a force 3 times that of the atom bomb.

Letting my imagination run wild produces several fears, one of which is that I'll have an idea that is outside of God's design. As if I will surprise God! If you approach creative

Staying on the Path

Be self-controlled and alert. Your enemy the devil prowls around like a roaring lion looking for someone to devour. Resist him, standing firm in the faith, because you know that your brothers throughout the world are undergoing the same kind of sufferings.

1 PETER 5:8-9

abundance by being available, by observing and expressing, what happens when you get a really wild idea? Do you just go for it? We want to be sure that it is from God. We do not want to allow our imagination to lead us off the path.

Our imaginations are not the playground for the devil. Certainly he is prowling around the jungle gym, but he is the single most predictable, unimaginative creature in all of existence. It is the oldest and worst lie that our imaginations belong to Satan.

Look back at the first three chapters of Genesis. Consider the scene in Genesis 2:19 when Adam is naming the animals. Compare that with Eve's conversation with the devil in Genesis 3:1-6. In her encounter with the snake, Eve is not being creative or using her imagination. She is listening to lies and staring at a forbidden tree, responding only to what she has surrounded herself with. If she took one step back and imagined death, or what God would say, or used any part of her capacity to think, she might have freed her gaze from the tree and her ear from the slick whispers of the evil one.

You have invited God into your imaginings, and you have created an environment for creativity, but that does not mean that lies, lust, vanity and temptations will not come your way. Those things are part of life. Keeping your creative life as a playground for you and your Lord will require that you maintain the context for creative living.

Tool

Only God creates from nothing. Our creativity comes from within a context. Look up these verses and use these evaluators to maintain a godly context for your creativity. Here are seven ways to analyze an idea to determine whether it is worth pursuing. If it is worth pursuing, your creativity will lead you closer to the heart of God.

1. Dig into the Word: Psalm 119:11 and Deuteronomy 11:18. Feed your creative life with the bread of life. Memorize Scripture. Read it out loud, taste it, hear it, see it, experience it. When Adam named the animals, he was talking to God. When Moses' mother put him in a basket and trusted him to the Nile, she was responding to God, not to Pharaoh or to the Nile (Exodus 2:3). Focus on God through his revealed Word.

2. *Worship God: John 4:24 and 1 Chronicles 16:28-29.* Throughout this book there are song titles. Use these songs to sing God's praises, to worship him for his character, not just for what he has done for you, but for who he is. If you do not know any of the suggested songs, open your Bible to the Psalms and start reading them aloud to God. Go to church and sing. Turn your imagination toward the source of creativity. Listen as you sing, and you will hear from him.

3. *Pray: Philippians 4:6-7 and Matthew 6:9-13.* Communion with God enriches every aspect of your life. Meditate on God's word and make your requests know to him. Sit quietly and listen. If you are his child you will recognize his voice.

4. *Look for the fruit: Galatians 5:16-26 and Malachi 3:2-4.* What is your creative life producing? What is your idea producing? Are you gratifying the desires of the sinful nature? Is your idea producing anxiety, impurity, immorality, fits of rage, hatred, jealousy, envy, drunkenness, lust or selfish ambition in you or anyone else?

Maybe the original idea does not produce any of those acts of the sinful nature, but maybe you are holding on too tightly to your idea and redirecting it. Invite the Spirit to purify your ideas and motives. Look for love, joy, peace, patience, kindness, goodness, faithfulness, gentleness and self-control. Ask God to infuse your creative life with the fruit of the Spirit. Ask God to refine your creativity.

5. *Say no: James 5:12 and 1 Peter 5:8-9.* If you are not ready to move forward, do not be afraid to say no. If your stomach is tightening, say, "My stomach is tightening, Lord; are you saying yes or no? If yes, then make me able to go there. If no, then give me the strength to say so."

Be soft and invite God into your fear. Tell him where you are: "God, I am not open to this," or "I want to be open here" or even "I do not ever want to be open to this." Invite God into where you are right now and ask him to make you

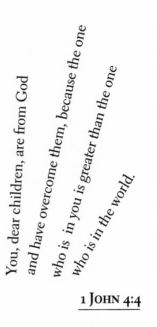

You, dear children, are from God and have overcome them, because the one who is in you is greater than the one who is in the world.

1 JOHN 4:4

willing to follow his lead. Ask him to protect you as you go. Be willing to say no to someone else or to yourself while you wait on him.

6. *Pretend to be your best friend: Matthew 22:37-40 and Proverbs 27:17.* Write down your idea and then walk away. Two days later look at it again and evaluate the idea as your best friend would.

If one of your friends asked you to read a short story he or she had written, you would look at it through eyes of love and admiration. You know your friends, you know their perspectives and intentions. You would build them up and encourage them. You would challenge them too. You would be excited about their idea because you know them and love them. Treat yourself the same way.

7. *Test the spirits: 1 John 4:1-6 and Galatians 1:10.* If you are unsure where your ideas are coming from, ask God. And ask yourself this question: "Who am I trying to please?" If your focus and desire is to please God, he will lead you. If you are trying to please everyone else first, then you are already off track, and that question will pull your focus back to him.

Creativity is a way to address the details of our lives and to allow the Holy Spirit to saturate every moment. So often we go about our lives as if nothing new and unique is happening; the laundry and the commute and the breakfast dishes and the unanswered e-mail give us that illusion. But we are eternal beings, and in every moment the Holy Spirit is permeating our reality and bringing forth new life.

Your creativity does not make you holy. It does not make your life more spiritual. Rather, it points you to the spiritual. Your imagination reminds you how very little you know about yourself, your thinking and the mind of God. "And he who searches our hearts knows the mind of the Spirit, because the Spirit intercedes for the saints in accordance with God's will" (Romans 8: 27).

A creative life is lived in excited anticipation for what God is doing in each moment. When we respond with imagination, we are reaching out and grabbing the hand of God, who is leading us to a deeper and richer life—a life

See, I am doing a new thing!
Now it springs up; do you
not perceive it.
I am making a way in the desert
and streams in the wasteland.

Isaiah 43:19

where Christ reigns in beauty, fear is banished and we are transformed into the full expression of our Lord and Savior.

Are you for abundant creativity? You will be as you worship. Read these verses aloud or write them in your journal.

Worship

> But you are a chosen people, a royal priesthood, a holy nation, a people belonging to God, that you may declare the praises of him who called you out of darkness into his wonderful light. (1 Peter 2:9)

> Praise be to the God and Father of our Lord Jesus Christ! In his great mercy he has given us new birth into a living hope through the resurrection of Jesus Christ from the dead, and into an inheritance that can never perish, spoil or fade—kept in heaven for you. (1 Peter 1:3-4)

Now sing to God:
"Jesus, What a Beautiful Name"
"As the Deer"
"You Have Been Given"

Expect your creative life to be beyond what you can ask or imagine.

Chapter 7

Creative Inspiration: Enjoying Abundant Thinking

> You welcome me as a guest,
>
> anointing my head with oil.
>
> My cup overflows with blessings.
>
> Surely your goodness and unfailing love will pursue me
>
> all the days of my life,
>
> and I will dwell in the house of the LORD
>
> forever.
>
> PSALM 23:5-6 NLT

*B*Y PLOWING THROUGH MANY OF THE FEARS WE have about creativity, we have primed ourselves and are now ready to receive abundance. Or are we? Life does not give us the tools to receive the beauty and abundance we long for. The habits we have developed are mostly defensive, to keep us from getting hurt. But the good news is that we can retrain ourselves to receive the overflow of creative inspiration God is sending our way.

Jars of Clay

Explore

In 2 Kings 4:1-7 we meet a woman who is good at receiving abundance. Turn there and delve into her story.

❏ Why was the woman in trouble?

❏ Why did she go to Elisha?

❏ Look at Elisha's instructions in verses 3-4. What do you think were the woman's thoughts and feelings on hearing this?

❏ What happened when there were no jars left?

❏ Given Elisha's response in verse 7, how much oil do you imagine the woman collected?

Imagine

Think about the widow's jars of oil. Now close your eyes and relax. Go back to the room of your heart and sit with the Lord. Don't be concerned if the room is altered a bit or even completely different. Today is a different day from the first day when you imagined the room of your heart.

Get comfortable in your heart's room.

Now imagine some empty jars. What size and shape are they? Are they new, or have they been there awhile? Are the jars colored or plain? Are they uniform, or is each one different?

Imagine that those jars represent different areas of your life: work, family, relationships with friends. Picture labels on them that relate to the roles you have in each of those areas. Touch some of the jars and see what their labels say.

Now offer to God the jars that you own, the ones you

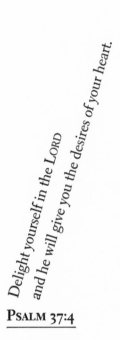

Delight yourself in the LORD and he will give you the desires of your heart.

PSALM 37:4

know well, and ask him to fill them with oil, his Holy Spirit.

Are there some jars without labels? Some may have had labels in the past, but you have held the jars too tightly and the labels have rubbed off. Some labels may have yet to be filled in. Offer to God the jars with labels that you cannot read, that are from your past or that will be filled in in the future—things that he has prepared in advance for you to do, which you do not yet see. Give God reign over all the areas of your life and ask him to fill them with the oil of his Spirit.

In chapter one we imagined our heart's room, and I shared with you the picture of the glistening, empty, wooden room that was my heart. That is not the end of the story.

A year after I pictured that empty room, my best friend, Clare, was in town from Los Angeles, and we spent the day talking, eating and praying. When she left that evening, I wanted to drink a cup of tea and sink into melancholy, but I had an overwhelming urge to read the Bible. I do not always listen to those urges, but I knew that if I did not respond to this one I would regret it.

I flipped open the Bible, thinking that if I wasn't that committed to reading it maybe I wouldn't see anything special, but God would not allow me to brush him off that day. The passage I read was 2 Kings 4. I was convicted that I needed to give my jars to the Lord and ask him to fill them.

I fell to my knees and prayed. I offered up all of the empty jars that I could think of—the jar of motherhood, my writing, being a wife, being a friend. I tried to examine each jar to make sure it was empty of pride, then I gave it to God to fill. This should have been a powerful moment, but it was not. I felt oddly distant from God, as if our business together was unfinished. I tried, but I could not think of any other empty jars to offer to him. So I walked away, wondering.

The next day was Sunday, and I was headed to church. I had forgotten all about my jars-of-clay time with God. I was not intrigued by the sermon title, "How to Handle the Transition You Are Going Through," because I was not in transition. Sure, my husband was. In a month he was going in for surgery to have a pituitary tumor removed from near his brain, and he had left his career as a professional actor and was now leading a drama ministry. However, I was still working at the theme parks, performing shows, being an actor, same old, same old. Okay, I had a new baby, but he wasn't that new—ten months old for heaven's sake!

I do not remember what songs we sang or what Scripture was read, but I do remember that at some point during the service I was flooded by the image of my heart as an empty room. Yes, I remembered that image and the sound of my clicking heels, but now there was something in the room with me: four clay jars filled neatly to the top with oil. They were big urns of the sort that you see in pictures of the Middle East, the kind I imagine were used at the wedding in Cana. Because they were big, I thought, for a split second, that I would be satisfied with those jars. Then I remembered that the oil stopped when the widow ran out of jars and that Elisha had said, "Don't ask for just a few." I could not believe that my God was calling me to abundance. In my heart I called out to him, "Fill the room! Stack jars on top of one another to the ceiling, and fill them with oil until it spills out!"

It is so difficult for me to receive. I have trained myself to be in charge and to handle everything. But as I asked for more, I felt God's pleasure. He was glad that I was not settling for only what I knew about myself. There are jars in that room whose labels I recognize—motherhood, writing, acting, loving. Then there are jars that I have no idea what they say. Some may be past events or hurts that God wants to redeem and use. Others may be future directions. All I know is that they are available to him, placed there for him, made by him and filled by him. My cup overflows and I will dwell in the house of the Lord forever.

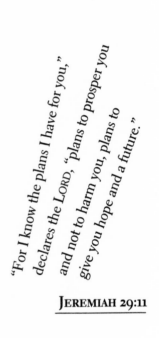

"For I know the plans I have for you," declares the LORD, "plans to prosper you and not to harm you, plans to give you hope and a future."

JEREMIAH 29:11

Under the Mercy

Therefore, I urge you, brothers, in view of God's mercy, to offer your bodies as living sacrifices, holy and pleasing to God—this is your spiritual act of worship. Do not conform any longer to the pattern of this world, but be transformed by the renewing of your mind. Then you will be able to test and approve what God's will is—his good, pleasing and perfect will.

ROMANS 12:1-2

Our fears about creativity are timid attempts to keep God at arm's length: if he pours out his abundance into our lives, we may not be able to control him. But if we participate in our creative life by taking in his beauty and offering up our beauty, we will be transformed and renewed. We may not even feel the need to control God.

A creative life is one that is continually offered to God. Giving our bodies to God, being used creatively by him, is possible only in view of his mercy. Risk is a part of creativity. Maybe no one will embrace your idea. Maybe no one will like it. Worse, maybe everyone will love it and more will be expected of you. The possibility of success and the threat of failure both produce strangling fears that keep us from participating, but in view of God's mercy we should offer our creativity, our very selves. Who cares if no one likes it? We are under the mercy. Who cares if everyone loves it? The focus of our offering is not our audience; the focus of our creative life is the Lord. And our offering, our living sacrifices, are holy and pleasing to him in view of his mercy.

Journal

❏ What are you longing to see happen in your life?

❏ Where is God saying no? Can you mourn the loss of that dream?

❏ How might God be reshaping your dream?

❏ How has God said yes to you in the past?

❑ How is he saying yes now?

❑ When you did the last Imagine exercise, had your heart's room changed?

❑ Which jars were difficult for you to hand over to God so he could fill them?

❑ What was your response to the jars being filled with oil?

My nutritionist told me that my cravings for Reese's peanut butter cups could be traced to a low blood sugar level. My craving is a signal from my body that I need a proper snack of protein (the peanut butter) and carbohydrates (the cup). I also wildly crave white corn tortilla chips with tons of salt. I decided not to ask my nutritionist about that. Instead I attribute it to a low white corn level, which means that I should eat tortilla chips whenever I fear that my level is dangerously low. But I bet both cravings reflect a deep desire for balance, for sweetness, substance and a zesty, crunchy life.

There is inspiration in our longings, and sometimes we can even discover God's dream for us there. Hear Jesus' heart cry when he calls out to Jerusalem in Matthew 23. Jesus longed to gather his people, knowing that they kill the prophets and stone those sent to them. This longing of

Longings and Promises

O Jerusalem, Jerusalem, you who kill the prophets and stone those sent to you, how often I have longed to gather your children together, as a hen gathers her chicks under her wings, but you were not willing.

MATTHEW 23:37

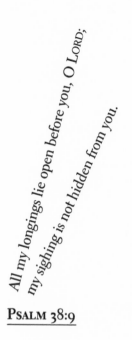

All my longings lie open before you, O LORD;
my sighing is not hidden from you.

PSALM 38:9

Jesus' provides deep insight into his life; this longing is why he came and why he died: so that he could gather his children to himself.

You may feel that your dreams have not been noticed by God, but look deeply at them to get a glimpse of how God is using some of those jars of yours.

God addresses our longings with his promises. Has God ever given you promises from his Word? Have you ever been in need and called out to him and had Scripture pop into your head?

The first time that happened to me I was fourteen years old. I had come across Proverbs 9:10: "The fear of the LORD is the beginning of wisdom, and knowledge of the Holy One is understanding." The verse resonated in my heart, and it became my desire to fear the Lord and to receive understanding.

Part of our inability to recognize God's promises in action is that we are looking at our dreams in relation to how the world rewards people. When you use your observing and expressing tool, you are training your mind to think on the things above, on what God is doing. Train yourself to look at every moment in the light of God's promises to see how he is answering.

Experience

Write down the promises in Scripture that are most meaningful to you, that God has given to you. If you do not feel that you have been given a promise, spend some time now meditating on God's word and ask God to give you a verse. If you do not have an emotional moment, do not despair; instead be obedient. Pick out a verse that is a promise about God's character and write it down.

On the left side of the page, write down the God's promises for you. Write the Scripture out, not just its verse number. Then on the right side of the page, write down your dreams and longings from your last journaling exercise. Look for the connection points. Ask God to reveal to you how he is shaping your dreams, how he is fulfilling your longings and how he wants to fulfill that to which he has called you.

God's Promises	My Dreams & Longings

God is speaking creatively to your heart in his Word. He is also inspiring you externally through your circumstances and through his creation. Train yourself to see all the areas in which God is revealing himself. When you know his Word you begin to see him revealed everywhere. When you understand that God is the original Thinker and the Author of creativity, you will recognize his signature in the creative works of others. If you want to be creative in your thinking, you need to allow yourself to be inspired by others' creativity.

Taking in the expression of others will challenge you. The resources for your creativity are not limited to your own creative life but are also found in the creative lives of others. The taste of peppermint, the scent of eucalyptus, the music of Bonnie Raitt, reading *A Wrinkle in Time*, watching an Albert Brooks movie, eating fresh scones and drinking hot tea—these are things that inspire me. When I soak them in I am lifted out of my old mental patterns, and I am moved to a new view.

Sometimes when I'm feeling low, unappreciated or just tired and bored, I get a *People* magazine and a pint of Ben and Jerry's ice cream. But the effect of this routine is the opposite of what I need. I am not lifted; rather, I sink deeper into the mire of boredom and self-cen-

Be Inspired

**Creative Inspiration
Reading List**

A Whack on the Side of the Head: How You Can Be More Creative, by Roger Van Oech (Warner Books, 1990).

Walking on Water: Reflections on Faith and Art, by Madeleine L'Engle (Harold Shaw, 1980).

Windows of the Soul: Experiencing God in New Ways, by Ken Gire (Zondervan, 1996).

Art and the Bible, by Francis A. Schaeffer (InterVarsity Press, 1973).

teredness. The shallow, glossy images affirm that I am the loser I thought I was, and I actively agree by slamming home some NY Super Fudge Chunk. Don't do that. If you see me doing it, tell me to stop. On second thought, don't. Just back away slowly; it could get ugly.

Taking in inspiration is good for you. It will lift you up. Taking in sludge will weigh you down. I cannot say it enough: If you are in Christ, you are safe to receive inspiration and to act on your own ideas. You know the difference between good and bad, and if you don't, God does, and he will separate the chaff from the wheat for you.

Celebrate the beauty around you and the inspiration given to others. Do not be afraid. If you are God's, you will recognize his handiwork, even in the work of people who say they don't know him. Their unbelief does not stop him from speaking through their creativity.

Journal

❑ What inspires you?

❑ What brings you down?

He has made everything beautiful in its time.
He has also set eternity in the hearts of men; yet they cannot fathom what God has done from beginning to end.

ECCLESIASTES 3:11

❑ List your favorite books, movies, music, places to go, foods, poems, plays, pictures and so on.

❑ In what areas of your life do you want or need inspiration?

While writing this book I have been reading like crazy. Coming from a performance background, I am used to going out and being applauded every twenty minutes. I receive tremendous inspiration from the input of our audiences. But as I write, I'm on my own; the only outside input I get is from Starbucks. Because I pray and read the Bible, I know that I am writing under God's influence, but I need human input. I need a connection with people who have gone before me, who know more than me, who are better writers than I am. Madeleine L'Engle, Edith Schaeffer, Natalie Goldberg, Anne Lamott, Aaron Sorkin, Thornton Wilder and Ken Gire—their input refreshes and affirms me, and I have something to say too! And back to the keyboard I go.

If you want to grow in your creative life, take in creativity. Get into the rhythm and the pattern of the lives of creative people who have shared and spoken about the things you are passionate about. See if the rhythm of their expression gets you out of your pattern and opens up new pathways for your creativity.

Tool

Go back to your journaling about the areas of your life in which you want to be inspired. Use some of our creative tools (metaphor, word jam, or timed journal) to discover where more inspiration can be found. Take three minutes and write.

❏ Read 1 Corinthians 15:35-44, 51-52. What happens to us when we experience physical death?

Explore

❏ List words Paul uses to describe our earthly bodies.

❏ List words Paul uses to describe our heavenly bodies.

❏ What is the difference between our earthly bodies and our heavenly bodies?

❏ In verse 41 what metaphor does Paul use?

Raw Materials

"This is what your Creator does. God loves you exceedingly, for you are God's creature and God gives you the best treasures, a vivid intelligence. Hence you must think every hour about how to make so great a gift as useful to others as to yourself by works of justice so that it will reflect the splendor of Sanctity from you and people will be inspired by your good example to praise and honor God."

HILDEGARD VON BINGEN
1098-1179

When I was a kid, we went from Idaho to Virginia by car four times. I loved seeing the change from the Rockies to the plains, to the cornfields of Iowa to the Blue Ridge Mountains. We were always stopping the car to get out and find driftwood, seashells, pine cones or shiny rocks for my mother's collection. She made a collage of seashells and polished rocks and arranged pine cones in the fireplace. A large piece of driftwood welcomed visitors to our home. It is a family tradition to yell when speeding down the highway, "I see a pine cone!"

One day we will be in heaven and we will have heavenly bodies. Our bodies will not be the way they are now, and there will be a new heaven and a new earth. I have no idea what that will be like, but I am pretty sure that we will not be making driftwood art in heaven. Now is the time for pine cones and seashells. This is your opportunity to enjoy the splendor of the earth and your earthly body.

Experience

Commit a creative act. Plant an herb garden. Make a flower arrangement. Paint by numbers. Make wind chimes. Draw a picture. Play with clay. Stencil a border. Bake a cake. Write a story. Translate an idea that is in your head, through your body, to the raw materials available to you now. Make something that gives you pleasure as you do it.

Don't worry about the finished product. Don't worry if it doesn't last. Enjoy the process. Do not make this creative act about perfection or artistry; instead make it an opportunity to redeem your creative rejection. If you were told you can't draw, than get out some crayons and construction paper. This is not for someone else to view. This is your moment to listen to the stirring in your soul and to respond physically to it. Get your hands dirty and enjoy it.

Worship God for how present he is in your life. Worship him because he is not a God who is distant, because he invaded humanity through Jesus Christ. He is invading your life right now. Worship him for the grace that bends down. Delight in the One who got his hands full of clay when he created humanity.

    Song suggestions:

"Amazing Grace"

"Lord Most High"

"This Is My Father's World"

"Of the Father's Love Begotten"

Worship

The heavens declare the glory of God; the skies proclaim the work of his hands.

PSALM 19:1

Chapter 8

Creative Living: A Masterpiece in Progress

> Jesus replied: " 'Love the Lord your God with all your heart and with all your soul and with all your mind.' This is the first and greatest commandment. And the second is like it: 'Love your neighbor as yourself.' All the Law and the Prophets hang on these two commandments."
>
> MATTHEW 22:37-40

*I*N PURSUING A CREATIVE LIFE WE HAVE DISCOVERED that each one of us has the nature of our Creator woven into our DNA. When you come to Jesus, you can expect redemption of your imagination and a continual flow of the expression of Christ through your creative life.

Being creative is not a method for self-focus. Creative living is boldly acknowledging who you are in Christ and submitting that wholeness to him, who then reveals himself to your neighbor, your block, your town and the world.

First and Second

I have naturally curly hair. Really, really curly. It was wavy when I was little, but when I hit the age of thirteen it frizzed out. Luckily for me, that was in the late 70s, and curly hair was in.

Another friend of mine had curly hair too, and when people would tell us how lucky we were, he would say, "Yes, God loves us." And yes, God does. But I see my hair about fifteen minutes a day. You see it much more than I do. If my hair is special to look at, that is for your enjoyment. It is special to me because it is easy. I am reminded that God loves me when my day is spent dropping off my son at school, dashing downtown for meetings, hurrying back to church to help Tim, grabbing Henry after school and taking him home to make dinner, all under a haze of Florida humidity. It makes me feel special that my hair does not look as frantic as I feel.

Our gifts are not simply an indication of how much he loves us; they are an indication of how much he loves. When you use your abilities to the fullest, earnestly desiring communion with God through the gifts he has given, the attention will go to him. The result will be to draw you into fellowship with him and his people.

❏ Read Matthew 22:37-40 and Deuteronomy 6:1-9. According to Jesus, what is the greatest commandment?

Explore

❏ What is the second greatest? Why?

❏ What do we learn in Deuteronomy 6:2 about why Moses was to teach the people the commands?

❏ What will the people experience if they are careful to obey?

❏ How was Israel to respond to the commandments?

❏ What would it be like to have this one command impressed upon your heart?

❏ How would this command motivate you in your relationships?

in your work?

in your life?

Loving your neighbor as yourself is a challenge. Sometimes we do not love ourselves very much. Sometimes we love ourselves a little too much. To live a creative life you need accurate self-esteem. My hope is that through this book you have learned to love and appreciate who you are, who God has made you and how he desires to fulfill you, his work of art. And if you have hold of this love for yourself, what do you do now? Love God with all your imagination, creativity, heart, mind, body and soul, and love your neighbor as yourself. Love God. Love your neighbor. And love yourself.

A Higher Angle

About three years into our marriage I began to believe that my husband was trying to drive me crazy. I would come into the kitchen after him and all of the dishtowels would be in damp heaps on the counter tops. Aaagh! Didn't he know they would mildew that way? I would hang them back on the cabinet handles and leave the kitchen. When I would return five minutes later, there they would be—up on the counters again. The thoughts in my mind ranged from "He is totally clueless" to "He doesn't care about me at all." Then I started tailing him to see if I could glare him into hanging up the towels. I came into the kitchen and there was my six-foot-two husband bent in half trying to get a towel from the handle under the counter. After he dried his hands, he placed the towel on the counter, reaching down to do that. When he left the kitchen, I picked up the towel and hung it on an upper cabinet handle, eye level for five-foot-two me, arm level for him. No more towel issues.

Your creative life is not fulfilled if it remains yours only; not only do you need to share your own perspective, but you also need to look at things from the angles of the people around you. As we appreciate the creative lives around us we are unified with one another. We count on others to fill in our weaknesses with their strengths, and we offer our abilities to extend someone else.

Imagine

Read John 6:1-15. Close your eyes and imagine the shore of the sea of Galilee. Picture the waves. Smell the air. Feel the damp air on your arms, the rocks under your feet. Imagine standing among the many people being hungry. Strain to hear and see Jesus as the daylight wanes. Now imagine the scene from different perspectives: Stand next to Phillip. What is he seeing? How might he be feeling as the food is distributed?

Now picture yourself with the family of the little boy. What motivated the boy to come forward? What might he be thinking as he sees the people being fed from his lunch? What about the boy's mother and father? Did they join him in coming forward, encouraging him on, or did they hang back in shock?

What is the five thousandth person seeing and experiencing, way at the back of the crowd? How hard is it to keep your attention on Jesus from back there? Is it easy to wait for the food? Are you nervous that it will run out, or are you at peace?

Now imagine being next to Jesus, on the mountainside. What does the crowd look like from his vantage point?

What is Jesus' perspective on the crowd? How does he feel about them? How does he feel about Phillip? about the boy? about the five-thousandth person?

Simmer

My creative process is like a spark set to a fuse. The flame licks the cord quickly, it reaches the powder keg, and ideas explode. There is very little energy left for follow-through. My husband is like a campfire packed with tinder and paper. The wood seems to take forever to light, then you notice there is smoke, and once the wood catches, it blazes steadily for a good long time.

Experience

List several people in your life and use the word jam tool to ponder whether their creative life simmers, sparks or percolates.

Name:

Creative process:

Name:

Creative process:

Name:

Creative process:

> For by him all things were created: things in heaven and on earth, visible and invisible, whether thrones or powers or rulers or authorities; all things were created by him and for him. He is before all things, and in him all things hold together.
>
> COLOSSIANS 1:16-17

❏ Do these people operate primarily in the creative phase or the productive phase?

❏ How can their ideas be fed?

❏ How are they inspired?

❏ How can they be motivated to action?

❏ What is a metaphor for your creative process?

Journal

❏ What is a metaphor for your coworker's creative process?

Just as each of us has one body with many members, and these members do not all have the same function, so in Christ we who are many form one body, and each member belongs to all the others. We have different gifts, according to the grace given us.

ROMANS 12:4-6

your boss's creative process?

your family members'?

your friends'?

❑ How does each metaphor help you to relate to each person's creative process?

Be imitators of God, therefore, as dearly loved children and live a life of love, just as Christ loved us and gave himself up for us as a fragrant offering and sacrifice to God.

EPHESIANS 5:1-2

The purpose of a creative life is to delight in the abundant life in Christ and to offer your expression in service back to him, for the glory of God and the building up of his people. Compare the body of Christ to art, and you will see a mosaic, a painting like Seurat's *Sunday in the Park* or the movie poster from *The Truman Show*. Each tiny individual piece of the body of Christ is beautiful and complete unto itself, but only when the pieces are joined together is the true beauty realized—a living, breathing portrait of Jesus, who is fully human, fully divine.

The Art of Living

In 1994 I heard author Cal Searfield's definition of art: "Art is to be like clothes. A gift of the Lord to cover our nakedness, to dress our human life with joy, to strengthen and enrich our labors of praising God, serving the neighbor and caring for the world." That definition changed my life. I began to love my work as an actor and desire to do it to the best of my ability. I wanted to offer a performance of such truth, sincerity, power, genuineness, warmth, wit, timing, creativity and uniqueness that it would draw people in, not to me or to the gift but to the Savior. My dream was that the response of an audience member would be "Only to the Lord, the Creator, the God of Israel, the God of history, the God of perfect timing, the God of compassion, the God who sees me, the God who sacrificed. Only he could speak like that to me through that girl. Only he could create that gift. Only he could fulfill it."

Make a list: What is the purpose of art for artists?
❏ to reveal their struggle
❏ to celebrate the Source
Keep going.

> Do not think that I have come to abolish the Law or the Prophets; I have not come to abolish them but to fulfill them.
>
> **MATTHEW 5:17**

What is the purpose of art for viewers?
❏ to be drawn in to another's pain, joy, triumph, hurt, perspective, understanding
❏ to relate to the expression of another's soul
Keep going.

It was Charlie Peacock who quoted Cal Searfield. Peacock was giving a talk for Ligonier Ministries that was originally titled "Where Are All the Great Christian Artists?" By the time he gave the speech, he had to change the title to "Where Are All the Christian Artists?"

Let me tell you a little secret about why good Christian art is hard to find and hard to create: We Christian artists are so concerned about reflecting Christ perfectly and precisely that we miss out on our opportunity to share how Christ is working in our hearts. We fear that if we express ourselves artistically, someone might see a bit of our struggle, and we will have ruined the viewer's chance to see Jesus.

We have the same fear in creative living. We are afraid that if we are creative we will not be able to be precise in our delivery of the gospel. It is impossible for you to express the entire gospel, the perfection of our Lord past, present and future in each moment of your life. Only Jesus was able to fulfill completely, in one life, all of the Law and the Prophets.

There were some four hundred years between the time when the last Old Testament prophet spoke and the time when John the Baptist proclaimed the advent of Christ. There were over four hundred years between Joseph's death and God's deliverance of Israel from Egypt. The Bible spans over a thousand years. It is impossible to express all of it in one painting, one play or one song.

What is the solution then? To live a free-spirited life and to not concern yourself with the gospel of salvation? Or to turn your back on creativity and try to express every jot of Scripture?

The solution is to play your role. Fully inhabit the part that God asks you to play in his eternal work. Be willing not to explain the depths of Christ, but rather to live to him, allowing him to reveal the vastness of Christ in your small offering. Allow your tiny offering to reveal your heart, to express your hurt, and allow God to speak the entire gospel through that moment.

> He also saw a poor widow put in two very small copper coins. "I tell you the truth," he said, "this poor widow has put in more than all the others. All these people gave their gifts out of their wealth; but she out of her poverty put in all she had to live on."
>
> LUKE 21:2-4

True Inspiration

As I think on the Deuteronomy 6 passage we explored earlier in this chapter, I am struck by the call to a creative life. If you and I were to impress God's Word on our hearts, if we were to be filled to all the fullness of Christ, out of us would spill God's life. How we serve dinner would impress the commandments on our children. The way in which we love the unlovable at work, making our toil excellent to the glory of God, would reveal his Word written on our hands and foreheads. Sharing our hearts and lives with our friends, neighbors, family and the PTA would reveal his commands as we are sitting at home, walking along the road, lying down and rising up.

We are called to do as Christ did, to submit ourselves to God, that he may take our lives and lift them through resurrection and fulfill them. God is our Creator, the Artist who fills in our lives with bold strokes. Before his birth, Jesus had it all. He reigned with the Father from the beginning, and through him all things were made. For us and for the Father's purpose he laid down his authority, his glory, and confined himself in the human form; the Artist filled in his sketch, his pencil drawing of humanity.

> Now we see but a poor reflection as in a mirror; then we shall see face to face. Now I know in part; then I shall know fully, even as I am fully known.
>
> 1 CORINTHIANS 13:12

Jesus our Messiah, our Lord, then laid down that life for us, for the Father's good plan. In doing this he was raised to the highest heights, to the right hand of the Father, where he is now, the link between the Creator and the created.

In laying down our lives we can expect the same process. Submission to Christ. Death of self. Fulfillment by God. We take the lump of clay of our lives, which is marred by sin, which we have been painstakingly, arduously trying to form into something beautiful and worthwhile, and we put it in the hands of our Maker. He shapes it, fulfilling his original design, his eternal plan. He brings beauty out of the clay, use from its form, and his work delights all who see and experience his artistry.

Charlie Peacock also defined the calling of the Christian artist: "The Christian artist's dream is to create art so beautiful, so compelling that it will attract and move people towards Jesus."

The Christian life is not one of replication. We cannot reproduce the life of Christ in us. Instead, we submit ourselves to him and ask him to live his life in us. When we continually give ourselves to him, as he gave himself for us, we allow him to be revealed in us. It is my dream, not just as an artist or as a woman but also as a child of God, to express the life of Christ in and through my work, my art and my relationships. And I think it is your dream too, to live so beautifully that your friends, your neighbors and your family are compelled to experience and express Jesus in their own lives. You have a consecrated creative life that will attract and move people toward Jesus.

Worship

Grab your pen and get ready to journal. Before you begin to write, sing one of these songs:
    "Lord Most High"
    "All Creatures of Our God and King"
    "How Can I Keep from Singing?"
    "O the Deep, Deep Love of Jesus"

Journal

Take a look back at the creative journey you have made, rereading your Journal and Imagine exercises.

❏ Where did you start out?

❏ How has your faith deepened?

❏ Where have you expanded?

❏ What differences do you notice from your first Imagine exercise to the most recent one?

❏ What was the metaphor for your creative life when you began, and what is the metaphor now?

❑ How does your creative life affect your walk with the Lord?

❑ How does your creative life affect your relationship with your family?

❑ How does it affect you at work or school?

❑ How do you feel about your creativity?

Put down your pen and close your eyes. Go again to your heart's room. Are you relaxed there? Ask God to join you. Enjoy his presence. Ask him what one thing he wants you to know at this moment. Ask him for a Scripture verse to memorize. Enjoy him.

When you get up to go, leave the door to your heart open so you can visit anytime.

Leader's Guide

The Creative Life *for Small Groups*

The Creative Life is a wonderful tool for small groups or for one-on-one mentoring. Your role as leader is not to unearth the creative life of each individual; rather, it is to create an environment that will foster imagination.

Leading the creative life is like leading a group out to a playground. You want to participate and have fun, but you also need to get people home on time with no injuries.

The Playground

One of the reasons some people are nervous about creativity is that nonbelievers have deified their imaginations and have made creativity a religion. There is a freedom, a joy and a connection that you feel when you use your imagination, but when you do not recognize the Source of your imagination, those experiences can be an end unto themselves.

You will need to foster an atmosphere in which imagination is kept in its proper role. Worship is where you can experience God's character, his Word is where you know his will, and prayer is where you commune with him. The Imagine exercises are not a place to hang your faith—"This is how I know God." Instead, imagination is a playground.

Be safe. Boundaries in a group allow people to relax. Simple things like beginning and ending on time, getting to all of the material in a meeting and providing a chance for everyone to participate fosters freedom instead of squelching it.

How can you get to all of the material in a chapter in a single meeting? Don't do all of the exercises during the group time. At the end of each meeting let people know which exercises you will do as a group the following week; that way they can set aside those exercises for your time together.

Play well with others. When you are real and vulnerable about your discoveries and your fears, that will set the tone for your group. Join in the Worship and Imagine exercises. Do not be tempted to watch from the sidelines.

Begin at the beginning. When you first meet, even if you already know each other it is good to share something that binds you together and that sets the stage for the type of group yours will be. Even if people have not acquired their books yet, you will want to use your first meeting to take them through the introduction and to let them know what to expect. When you invite them to come, ask them to bring a Bible verse that says something about what they are going through in their life right now. Or ask them to bring their favorite quote on creativity to share. You can open the meeting with everyone's verse or quote, then read aloud together Psalm 108 from *The Message* (you'll find it at the beginning of the introduction).

At each of the subsequent meetings, you can dissolve any nervousness about who will speak up first by opening with a group activity. Try the Worship suggestions or read some of the Scriptures aloud together. You can also invite people to share which of the stories in the chapter spoke to them most and why. Once you feel ready to focus, do so by praying.

At the end of your meetings you may want to worship together. Don't worry about your singing ability or musical accompaniment; just pick a song and a note, and sing to the Lord.

Your Focus

It's a good idea to know your purpose for each meeting time. That way no matter where the discussion goes you can bring it back when you need to. In this appendix you will find an outline that you can fill in to help you lead the group. Where it says "My focus," you can write a sentence that describes your aim for the meeting. It may be as simple as "I want everyone to feel comfortable," or as intense as "I want Christ's renewing presence to be felt." This becomes your prayer for your meeting and for each person through the week.

It is important that you pray for each person during the week. You might even want to e-mail or call them a few days before you meet to maintain the sense of community that is so necessary for creative growth.

The key to leading the Imagine exercise is to treat it as a prayer. Begin by reading aloud the Scripture that is connected to the exercise, and invite people to close their eyes and relax. Try to relax yourself by speaking in a soft tone and taking your time. You can read a few of the lines and then close your eyes and imagine too. If you are using your imagination, it will be easier to lead others because you will be in step with the exercise and fully participating.

You will want to pray silently while you are leading the exercise. Ask for God's leadership. Then you will know when to move on to a new image and when to linger. Ask him to help you to be sensitive to what he is doing in the imaginations of those around you. Often I am tempted to think, "This is stupid. I'm sitting here with my eyes closed and they are all staring at me and wishing I would be quiet." That is not what is happening. I have led small groups of five and congregations of a hundred and fifty people. Each time has been a profound encounter with the Lord. Even people who do not participate are respectful of the courage and the delight that others are exhibiting.

After you finish the last part of the exercise, leave some time for people to simmer a bit. Then simply pray to end the exercise. On occasion you may want to begin one of the songs or read one of the perimeter Scriptures to close the exercise. You began by focusing on God. If you finish that way, you create a soft ending rather than jarring everyone back to reality.

People will want to share what they discovered during their Imagine exercises. I was invited speak at a young adult service, and I ended our time together with the heartroom imagining. For a month the halls were buzzing with

Leading the Imagine Exercise

twenty-somethings asking, "What did your room look like?"

For the first couple of meetings you will want to do the Imagine exercise toward the end of your meeting, then invite people to share their experiences the following week. Make it clear that it is not mandatory for everyone to share their experience. When you've reached chapter three or four, you can invite people to share during that session what their garden or city was like. Your group will let you know if they want to share their imaginings right away or if they need a week to process.

The Chapters

You can take each chapter and go through it as it is laid out, or you can pick and choose which exercises and stories you want to touch on during each session. The best exercises to do together are the Tool, Worship and Imagine exercises. Some of the Experience exercises may also be appropriate as a group activity. You will want to touch on the Explore and Journal exercises by picking one or two questions to highlight.

You may want to create an outline for each session with the following elements:

My Focus:
Opening:
Explore highlight:
Journal highlight:
Exercise together:
Closing: